CH00663722

THE RIVER A. ~..

Navigation Guide & Visitor Guide
River Avon between Tewkesbury and Alveston
1st Edition 2009

Compiled and revised by Dudley Matthews MBE
who gratefully acknowledges the help and assistance given by members of
the Reach Masters and Associates,
Philip Bidwell, Pat Dodson, Clive Matthews, Wyn Matthews and Robin Smithett

Published by

AVON NAVIGATION TRUST

Registered Office: Mill Wharf, Mill Lane, Wyre Piddle, Pershore, Worcestershire WR10 2JF
Telephone: 01386 552517
Registered Charity Number: 244951
2009

Photography: Robin Smithett

Printed by John Knight Press, Pershore

ISBN Number: 978 0 9562289 0 1

INDEX

Pershore Great Bridge

INTRODUCTION

The statutory Navigation Authority for the River Avon between Tewkesbury and Alveston is the Avon Navigation Trust. The Navigation of the River Avon is independent; it is not nationalised, nor part of British Waterways' navigations, nor of any other body operated by the state; its Navigation is not controlled in any way by any other water or river authority.

The Avon Navigation Trust, a non-profit making registered charity, was formed by the amalgamation of The Lower Avon Navigation Trust Limited and The Upper Avon Navigation Trust Limited. The Lower Avon Navigation Trust Limited was founded in 1950 to take over the semi-derelict navigation of the Lower Avon from its confluence with the River Severn at Tewkesbury to Evesham Lock, to restore it to navigability and to run it. The Upper Avon Navigation Trust Limited was founded in 1965 to restore the Upper Avon from Evesham Lock through Stratford upon Avon to Alveston. The legal objects of the Avon Navigation are "... to maintain and improve the Navigation ...". It is controlled by a Council elected each year by its members; anyone can become a member on payment of a minimum annual subscription. Its Council embraces people with a very wide range of expertise and experience, none of whom receive payment for their services and all of whom are dedicated enthusiasts. Its few officers and residential lock keepers share the same enthusiasm, receiving only very modest remuneration for their services.

Being an independent waterway means that the navigation of the Avon is run by volunteers and staff who know their river and its needs so that its operating costs are minimal.

Navigation is only a part of the river's function. Land drainage, water abstraction for irrigation of crops, angling, and the control of pollution (all of which are the Environment Agency's responsibilities) are essential elements of river usage. The river and its navigation are for the use and enjoyment of all. Footpaths and Ordnance Survey Map Numbers are included in this guide to help those who wish to enjoy walking near the river.

The Avon Navigation Trust (sometimes referred to in this book as "the Trust") welcomes all boat users to its river. It asks them to remember three points: that they are only a part of those using and enjoying its water; that the registration fees they pay for the use of the river are all spent on running the Navigation; and that all those who help on the Navigation are doing so because they believe that an independent member-controlled navigation is in the best interests of the River Avon.

WARNING

The Avon Navigation is a RIVER navigation, and is liable to flood during and after heavy or prolonged rainfall. At these times water levels can rise and the rate of flow (current) increases very rapidly, which may not always be obvious, thus turning the river into a serious potential hazard for users. When in doubt, stop, moor your craft securely and seek advice from lock keepers, boatyards or in the case of hirers from the yard from which you hired your boat. The Association of Pleasure Craft Operators in collaboration with the Environment Agency has set up a network of Navigation Hazard Warning Signs which advise against moving when the river rises above a certain level. Hired craft are expected to follow this advice which should be considered by all craft. It can be DANGEROUS to navigate under adverse conditions. All Avon locks have water level gauges fitted at the lower end of the lock, as a flood warning system. If in any doubt about the level of the river, these should be consulted.

HEALTH AND SAFETY MISSION STATEMENT

The Avon Navigation Trust wishes to provide a welcoming and safe environment for all who use or work on our Navigation.

Our aim is to make sure that there are levels of safety at least as good as those found elsewhere for comparable activities.

The Trust's main concern is to prevent hazards arising, but, if we cannot do this, we will assess the risks to anyone who may be affected by our activities or from the assets under our control and work to eliminate or make the risks as low as is reasonably practicable to protect people from those hazards and prevent personal injury.

NAVIGABILITY

Where the metric equivalents to the Imperial measurements used in this handbook are not shown, reference should be made to the conversion figures below.

1 cm	= 10 mm	= 0.3937 in
1 m	= 100 cm	= 1.0936 yds
1 km	= 1000 m	= 0.6214 mile
1 in	= 2.54 cm	
1 ft	= 12 in	= 30.48 cm
1 yd	= 36 in	= 0.9144 m
1 mile	= 1760 yds	= 1.6093 km

The sizes and shapes of the locks vary but all craft within the dimensions 70 ft/21.3 m long, 13 ft 6 in/4.1 m beam and 4 ft/1.2 m draught can navigate the Lower Avon (downstream of Evesham) and craft within the dimensions 70 ft/21.3 m long, 12 ft 9 in/3.88 m beam and 3 ft/.914m draught can navigate the Upper Avon. (See para 12 page 9.) Dimensions of wheelhouses, dinghy davits, etc must be watched because of bridges where height and beam above the waterline are restricted. King John's Bridge, Tewkesbury, gives the least clearance or air draught and is considered to be the "gauge" bridge for the navigation up to Bidford Bridge, after which refer to appropriate diagrams.

With the exception of Tewkesbury the mill ponds and backwaters immediately upstream and downstream of the locks, weirs and sluices are either non-navigable (marked X on the charts) or are in private ownership and should not be entered unless taking up a mooring or visiting a boatyard.

ELECTRIC POWER LINES cross over the Avon at a minimum height above NORMAL SUMMER RIVER LEVEL of 30 ft/9.15 m.

Due allowance must be made for any variation of river level at time of semi-flood, also for a margin of safety against the possibility of flash discharge.

IT IS ESSENTIAL that craft navigating the Avon should NOT EXCEED an overall height from waterline to tip of mast, flag stay or the like of 30ft/ 9.15m for navigating at normal summer river level, and less than that at times of semi-flood, but should be prepared to lower masts.

DANGER

Electric power lines crossing the River Avon may not be at the minimum level. Sailing craft should proceed with caution.

Owners or hirers of craft ignoring these precautions travel the waterway at their peril.

TELEPHONE WIRES crossing the Avon have, in most instances, been raised to heights approaching those of electric power lines but no measurement can be given.

RULES AND REGULATIONS

Owners or hirers of boats using the Avon Navigation do so at their own risk and the Trust will not accept responsibility for damage or injury to boats or their crews whilst using the Navigation.

Rule of the River

In accordance with Maritime Conventions, the rule is to pass port to port (keep to the right), but always give way to cargo and maintenance craft which must be given priority at locks. One blast on your siren means that you are altering course to starboard (right), two blasts that you are altering course to port (left) and three blasts that your engines are going astern. One prolonged blast followed by two short blasts indicates that a vessel is approaching which may require the full width of the river to manoeuvre. Regulations as defined by International Maritime Law for prevention of collisions at sea also apply, and for this purpose the Navigation is deemed to be a narrow channel. (Byelaw 18(3))

Speed Limit

Persons using the Avon Navigation must at all times comply with the Byelaws, in particular that relating to the speed of craft which is as follows:

Speeding -

(1)   No person, being the navigator of a vessel propelled by an internal combustion engine, shall cause or suffer such vessel to exceed a speed of 6 miles per hour downstream and 4 miles per hour upstream over the bed of the river, (a fast walking pace).

(2)   In this context "navigator" means the person who, whether as owner or otherwise, has the charge or control of a vessel and includes any person who, being present, is entitled to give orders to the person having charge or control.

Water Ski-ing - No person shall engage in water ski-ing or any similar activity on the river.

Moored Craft - Speed should be reduced when passing moored craft so as not to cause inconvenience or possible damage to them.

Wash - At no time should a wash be created which may damage river banks or other craft.

BYELAWS

This is only an extract from the Byelaws of the Avon Navigation Trust (a copy of which is available for inspection at both lock keepers' offices during working hours or which may be purchased on application to the Company's Registered Office or on the Trust's website: www.avonnavigationtrust.org). The Byelaws are 42 in number and are therefore too numerous to set out in full here. You are advised to inspect a full copy of the said Byelaws. ANY PERSON CONTRAVENING THE SAID BYELAWS IS LIABLE TO PROSECUTION.

BYELAW 5
Certificate of Registration

A person shall not by himself, his servant or agent, launch, use or navigate or permit or knowingly cause to be launched, used or navigated or assist in launching, using or navigating any vessel (other than a tender to a vessel for which there is a Certificate of Registration in force) upon the Navigation unless a Certificate of Registration relating to the vessel be then in force.

BYELAW 6
Certificate of Registration to be exhibited

(1) Any vessel (other than a tender to a vessel for which there is a Certificate of Registration in force) kept on or launched upon the Navigation shall have exhibited and fixed to the vessel so as to be visible from the outside a Certificate of Registration then in force.

(2) The Master of every vessel shall produce on demand to any person duly authorised by the Trust or to any Police Constable the Certificate of Registration then in force in respect of that vessel.

Bidford Bridge

BYELAW 7
Name and identity of vessels
Every vessel shall have exhibited on the outside thereof so as to be clearly legible at all times at a distance of twenty yards and visible from both sides thereof, her name, or if unnamed, the name of her owner or a number allotted to her by the Trust for the purpose of identification except that a mark, name or number approved by the Trust and displayed on the sail or such other part of an unpowered pleasure boat as may be approved by the Trust may be accepted by the Trust as sufficient means of identification of such unpowered pleasure boat. In addition every vessel hired to other than the owner shall similarly exhibit the name and address or telephone number of the owner. A tender shall have exhibited the name or the number of her parent vessel or of her owner preceded by the words "tender to".

BYELAW 10
Vessels to have fenders lifebuoys ready for use
(1) Every sailing vessel over eighteen feet in length or power-driven shall have fitted adequate bow and stern fenders and have ready for immediate use other fenders of suitable material and in good condition and the Master of such vessel shall use such fenders whenever there is a risk of the vessel striking against any other vessel or against any wall, lock gate, bridge or other thing.

(2) Every vessel not otherwise required to carry life-saving apparatus except oared racing craft shall have ready for use a lifejacket or similar apparatus for each person carried or a lifebuoy of suitable material and in good condition for every two passengers or crew.

BYELAW 12
Fire extinguishers
(2) All powered vessels and all vessels equipped with non-electric apparatus for cooking, heating or lighting shall carry adequate fire appliances including at least one portable fire extinguisher of a type suitable for quenching oil, petrol or LPG fires.

BYELAW 13
Speed of vessels
(1) No vessel shall exceed 4 miles per hour when travelling upstream and 6 miles per hour when travelling downstream on any part of the Navigation not subject to local speed restrictions.

(4) Every vessel shall proceed at slow speed not exceeding 4 miles per hour when passing moorings, small craft and vessels not under way and those exercising fishing rights and when entering or leaving locks or lock cuts.

BYELAW 17
Master to be a responsible person
Every vessel when under way shall have a person in charge thereof as Master and no person shall (except in a case approved in writing by the Trust) permit a child under fourteen years of age to navigate any power-driven vessel unless there is an adult person supervising such navigation.

BYELAW 37
Master to obey directions
The Master of every vessel shall obey and conform to the directions of any officer of the Trust or of the water (river) authority or any Police Constable relating to the navigation, mooring or unmooring of such vessels.

Amongst other things the Byelaws also cover the following subjects:

8 Duty to supply information. 9 Conditions of vessels. 11 Stowage of equipment. 14 Engines to be silenced. 15 Noise. 16 Disposal of rubbish. 18 Rule of the river. 19 Sound signals. 20 Navigation of pleasure boats. 21 Vessels turning. 22 Navigation at night. 23-27 Locks and bridges and restrictions on navigation. 28-30 Mooring and use of vessels. 31-36 and 38-42 Many general provisions such as the creation of obstructions to navigation, prohibition of the use of firearms, shotguns or airguns from any vessel, prohibition of bathing in locks or lock cuts and the removal of derelict vessels from the Navigation.

These Byelaws should be read in conjunction with and subject to General Public Legislation and attention is drawn particularly to The Criminal Damage Act 1971; The Wildlife and Countryside Act 1981; Section 87 of the Environmental Protection Act 1990; The Public Order Act 1986 and The Merchant Shipping Act 1979 which refers to restricted navigation of a large vessel in a narrow channel as is this Navigation.

MOORING IN LOCK APPROACHES

Particularly on the Lower Avon, downstream of Evesham, mooring at lock landing stages and in lock approach channels is permitted only when locking and at no other time. They must not be used for short stay or overnight moorings as craft equipped with navigation lights may be travelling after dark and many move during the early hours. Also, often these stages are sited on privately owned land and thus subject to an undertaking that mooring other than for locking purposes will be prohibited.

REGISTRATION OF CRAFT

1.   All craft are required to comply with the Boat Safety Scheme and to be adequately insured.

2.   Details of current registration charges and Certificates of Registration may be obtained from the lock keepers at Avon Lock, Tewkesbury, and Evesham Lock or from the TIC in Stratford, Avon Boating in Stratford or the Registered Office, including reduced tolls under any reciprocal arrangements in operation with British Waterways.

3.   The Certificate of Registration is not transferable from one boat to another. It passes with the boat if it changes hands.

4.   Powered craft over 15 ft/4.6 m in length with a tender marked with the name of the parent vessel are permitted to use the Navigation without further charge for one such tender per vessel.

GENERAL INFORMATION
Essential Equipment for all Craft

1.   Bow and stern fenders of sufficient size. (Byelaw (10)(1))

2.   Life saving equipment. (Byelaw 10(2))

3.   Fire extinguishers. (Byelaw 12(2))

4.   At least two adequately stout lines of a minimum length of 30 ft/10 m ready for immediate use, one each at bow and stern.

5.   An anchor made off to a chain and/or warp permanently fixed to the boat, for use in the event of engine failure.

6.   For movement after dark, port, starboard, stern and masthead or centre lights; a single white light applies   to small craft and cargo carrying narrowboats only. (Byelaw 22)

OPERATING LOCKS

Landing stages have been provided at both the upstream and downstream ends of the locks. Particularly downstream of Evesham, mooring at these stages may be permitted only when locking.

The procedure of locking consists of this sequence of operations. WHEN LOCKING TO A HIGHER LEVEL: Open both bottom gates. The craft then enters the lock and makes fast with fore and aft lines ashore, keeping these constantly adjusted to take in the slack. Use of a centre line only is not considered to be adequate. The entry gates are then closed, and the rack gearing wound down to close the paddles. The rack gearings in the other pair of gates are then raised - at first a little way only, then, when the turbulence eases, to full open position - thus permitting water to enter the lock and raise the craft. As the craft rises, tighten ropes. Leave both exit gates open and all paddles closed.

WHEN LOCKING TO A LOWER LEVEL: Open both top gates. The same procedure as above is applicable. However, before drawing paddles, ensure that no craft is manoeuvring immediately downstream of the bottom gates. Boats should still be secured by ropes which should not be made off but paid out as the boat descends. Take care that all vessels are kept clear of the top cill as the lock empties. When the water level within the lock has dropped to the outer level, both the gates can be easily swung open.

Should the lock level be against the craft upon arrival, the lock will have to be emptied or filled as the case may be, by employing the above procedure before the craft can enter the lock. Leave both exit gates open and all paddles closed.

INCIDENTS AND ACCIDENTS

Problem with a boat or the gates -
CLOSE ALL PADDLES IMMEDIATELY then take the appropriate remedial action.

Someone falls in -
CLOSE THE PADDLES IMMEDIATELY.
Make sure boat engines are out of gear.

Shout to stop boats entering the area and to alert everyone nearby.

Use the lifebuoy to get flotation support to the person in the water.

If outside the lock, help them to the landing stage.

If in the lock, get the person to a fixed ladder.

If a boat has to be used in the rescue, ensure the propeller is nowhere near the individual.

Tewkesbury Abbey

Narrowboat descending Avon Lock, Tewkesbury

LOCK KEYS OR WINDLASSES

Lock keys must be carried in order to operate the paddles at unmanned locks. These keys may be purchased from the lock keepers at Avon Lock, Tewkesbury, and Evesham Lock or at most boatyards. All paddle gear accepts the 1 in (2.5 cm) taper BCN or Northwich type windlass or lock key; on double-ended keys, use the smaller taper.

LOCK KEEPERS' HOURS

At locks which are operated by resident lock keepers the duty hours for 2009* are as follows:

SUMMER PERIOD:

24th March - 20th April:	9 am - 6 pm
21st April - 31st Aug:	9 am - 8 pm
1st Sept - 31st Oct:	9 am - 6 pm

LUNCH BREAK:

12.45 pm - 2 pm (Last locking: 12.45 pm)
During this time Evesham and Avon locks are padlocked unless special arrangements have been made.

SURCHARGES:

Lock Keeper Hours may be further extended by prior booking and payment as follows:
8 am - 9 am: £5 per boat per lock if booked by previous day.
After normal duty for one hour: £5 per boat per lock if booked by 5 pm.
From 1 hour after normal duty to 8 am next day: £10 per boat per lock.

Volunteer members of the Trust and others undertake duties at all locks where resident lock keepers are not available during the period from about June 1st to September 30th* on most Sundays and Bank Holidays.

WINTER PERIOD:

1st November 2009 - 22nd March 2010*.
During this period lock keepers may be absent but locks are set for manual operation and crews of licensed craft may use them at any time.

*NOTE:

For subsequent years the actual starting and finishing dates for each period may vary by a day or so but will follow the same pattern and also the surcharges may alter. Latest information may be obtained from the residentially manned locks at Tewkesbury and Evesham or the Registered Office.

PLEASE TRY NOT TO DISTURB THE LOCK KEEPERS DURING THE MID-DAY BREAK

OVERNIGHT MOORING SITES

The Council of the Trust appreciates that there is a real need for suitable moorings, spaced throughout the length of the Navigation, where boats can moor for the night without interference. Because, particularly downstream of Evesham, the river banks are privately owned, or are occupied by non-boating interests, and there being no towpath, the problem is not easily or quickly solved. However, great progress is being made and successful negotiations have produced some sites, and efforts will continue to seek further likely areas. The situation can be improved if boaters consider other river users by making the maximum use of space available, eg closing up on other craft on the mooring and breasting up where possible, but please do not moor beyond the indicated limit of the mooring.

Only those moorings at present (2009) available are shown on the charts, and the limits of the bank within which craft should moor may be indicated by posts painted in the Trust's standard colour - Wedgwood blue - or where signs indicate.

Overnight mooring sites provided by the Trust or the local authorities are situated at: Tewkesbury (by arrangement with the lock keeper), Strensham Lock Island, Eckington Wharf, Birlingham Quay, Comberton Quay, Defford Road Wharf, Pershore Bridge Picnic Place, Pershore Lock Island (downstream), Pershore Recreation Ground (King George's Field), Wyre Lock Island (upstream), Craycombe Turn (between Fladbury and Chadbury locks), Waterside, Evesham Borough Workman Gardens, and Evesham Island (by arrangement with the lock keeper), Offenham Lock, Harvington New Lock, Bidford, Barton Lock, Bidford Grange Lock, Welford Lock, Binton Bridges, Luddington Lock, Weir Brake Lock, Stratford Trinity Lock and Stratford upon Avon.

The following boatyards etc may be able to provide overnight moorings for the appropriate fee, but prior arrangements are advised.

TEWKESBURY

Black Bear Inn	01684 292202
Severn Leisure	01684 593112
Tewkesbury Marina	01684 293737

TWYNING

Fleet Inn	01684 274310

PERSHORE

Angel Hotel	01386 552046
Star Inn	01386 552704

WYRE PIDDLE

Anchor Inn	01386 552799

EVESHAM

Sankey Marine	01386 442338

BIDFORD

Bidford Boats	01789 773205

BARTON

Barton Cruisers	01789 772003

WELFORD

Welford Boat Station	01789 750878

STRATFORD UPON AVON

Stratford Marina	01789 778358

Mooring at designated lock landing stages and in lock approach channels is permitted only when locking and at no other time, particularly downstream of Evesham. (See page 9.) Also at Pershore, Wyre and Chadbury where the only access is by boat, there is a mooring on the upstream side of the lock island which is reserved for the Duty Lock Keeper or other Trust workers on official business and must be kept clear at all times.

NAVIGATION

The Avon, being a river navigation, is unlike canals in that the water is not static but is "running water" and constantly moving with a considerable variation in its rate of flow, while levels can change quickly - even overnight. This and the following points should be borne in mind particularly by all those more accustomed to the canal system, and captains of narrowboats which, on account of their size and weight, can easily get into difficulties and possibly cause damage to river installations or other craft, and increase the costs to the Trust of maintaining the "navigability" of the river.

1.   Allow ample time for stopping. When travelling downstream where possible turn upstream into the current as immediately a vessel ceases to move at a speed greater than the rate of flow of water, steerage is lost.

When stopping always use the engine and NEVER use the lock gates, chambers, abutments or landing stages to bring the boat to a stop. Similarly damage can be caused to the river bank and landing places by running the bow of a heavy boat into them. Once again - ALWAYS USE THE ENGINE TO STOP THE BOAT.

When travelling downstream do not attempt to turn immediately upstream of a bridge, go through and turn. CRAFT NAVIGATING UPSTREAM SHOULD GIVE WAY TO THOSE TRAVELLING DOWNSTREAM.

2.   Most weirs are long, high and unprotected with adjoining variable sluices. Therefore, when approaching a lock from upstream, reduce speed early but keep steerage way on until clear of the weir crest or sluice channel.

3.   Be equipped with at least two adequate stout lines at least 30 ft/10 m long - ready for use, one at the bow and the other at the stern.

4.   Have an anchor ready in the event of engine failure. If power is lost a boat may well NOT drift into the bank, but be carried by the stream on to the next downstream weir, or over it if there is sufficient flow of water.

5.   Summer floods can build up in a matter of hours. Under these conditions especially a lower powered or heavier canal craft can again get into difficulties so, if in doubt, turn into the stream, moor up, and wait for the water to drop. It is possible to wind (turn) a full-length boat practically anywhere on the main river.

6.   Unlike on the narrow canal system, bumper, mitre and breast plates are not fitted to any of the cills or gates, nor are there any strapping posts on the gates although some do have facing planks. If it is necessary, on account of length, to hold the boat against the top gates when locking up, ensure that the fore end, which MUST be equipped with an adequate bow fender, rests on the mitre posts and does not catch under the horizontal cross beams or other parts of the gates or their fittings as this could result in lifting a gate off its pintle. FOLLOW RIVER PRACTICE WITH FORE AND AFT LINES ASHORE, KEEPING THESE CONSTANTLY ADJUSTED TO TAKE IN THE SLACK. Use of a centre line only is not considered to be adequate. Do NOT use the boat to force open lock gates, nor slam a set of gates by raising paddles at the other end.

7.   When filling the locks (which unlike narrow canal locks are much broader than the boat, and, except for Avon Lock at Tewkesbury and Pershore Lock, equipped only with gate paddles) considerable turbulence can be expected when the paddles are raised. Initially a little at a time is recommended, using first the paddle in the gate on the same side as that to which the boat is tied.

8.   It is not necessary to close the gates on leaving a lock apart from the upstream gates at Avon Lock (see para 9 below). However, it is considered to be courteous to lower the paddles - gently.

Nafford Lock with the swing bridge visible on the right

Avon Lock, Tewkesbury

9.   AVON LOCK, Tewkesbury: A post by the ground paddle at the upstream end of the lock on the house side may be used with a length of line from the fore end stud to assist in turning upstream, ie left after having locked up. On the opposite side there is a height gauge showing the clearance under King John's Bridge with the water level as it is when leaving the lock.

The upstream gates, which incorporate a footbridge, must be left closed, and the chain which prevents them swinging open replaced.

10.   NAFFORD LOCK: A line from the bow to the post on the upstream corner of the hut side of the lock may be required to facilitate the right hand turn after locking up.

11.   PERSHORE LOCK: DRAW THE GROUND PADDLE FIRST when locking up; do not draw the top gate paddles until they are submerged.

12.   CHADBURY and EVESHAM LOCKS: Although 14 ft/4.3 m wide these locks are rather short between the top cill and the bottom gates at low summer level. This may make them a bit tight, lengthways, for certain types of full-length narrowboats and barges (see para 15) but alterations to the shape of the cills have been made to give more clearance for a single long boat positioned in the centre of the lock. It may be advisable when locking down to have the boat in the lock stern end downstream to avoid the risk of damage to the helm or screw on the top cill, but, if so, to avoid the risk of the screw washing silt or other obstructions onto the cill rendering the lock inoperable, the engine should not be engaged in the vicinity of the gates. The boat should be warped into or out of the lock on lines.

13.   HARVINGTON LOCK: Proceed with care upstream of the lock to avoid shallows and weir on the right.

14.   MARLCLIFF LOCK: Proceed with care when navigating at summer levels keeping to the right for 1000 yards/914.4m upstream of the lock to avoid shallows.

15.   The locks on the Avon can accommodate boats of 70 ft/21.3 m in length. This is an advised maximum and includes an adequate bow fender which is ESSENTIAL when navigating the river. It may be necessary to raise this and/or the tip-cat fender in order to give clearance when swinging the gates, but these must be set back in place after clearing the lock. The same rules apply to a towed butty. Slightly longer craft in the hands of experienced skippers may be able to passage the locks, subject, of course, to the river levels appertaining at the time, but extreme care is essential and the attempt should be aborted if damage is likely to be caused to the Navigation's installations.

16.   At present (2009) there are dry dock facilities at Harvington (to be booked through the Trust's office), Gloucester Docks, Worcester (Diglis), and Stourport on Severn.

ADVICE AND ASSISTANCE

Should you require advice or assistance on any matter relating to the Navigation, the lock keepers at Avon Lock, Tewkesbury and Evesham Lock and skippers of vessels flying a swallow-tailed Trust flag edged red are experienced officers of Avon Navigation Trust who are willing to assist.

SAILING

Some parts of the river are used for dinghy sailing and on most weekends races are organised by the various clubs which are based on certain reaches. Care should be exercised in order to avoid any course buoys and markers
and consideration be shown to competitors. It is however emphasised that the Navigation is deemed a narrow channel throughout its length.

Under normal circumstances it is usually best to endeavour to maintain at a fixed speed a steady course to starboard by keeping to the right hand side of the channel.

The areas in which the sailing clubs are situated and where racing takes place are:

TEWKESBURY
The Tewkesbury Cruising and Sailing Club for about one mile above the Clubhouse.

BREDON
The Severn Sailing Club for about one and a half miles downstream from the watermain pipe bridge past the Clubhouse.

ECKINGTON
Arden Sailing Club for about one mile downstream of the railway bridge.

WYRE PIDDLE
Wyre Mill Club between the mill and Pershore Recreation Ground.

EVESHAM
Evesham Sailing Club immediately upstream of Evesham weir.

CANOEING
Touring canoeing is becoming increasingly popular. On the competitive side of the sport the River Avon caters for slalom and wild water enthusiasts and is ideal for marathon racing. At least two major marathon races are held each year at Fladbury and at Tewkesbury.

Organised canoe clubs are becoming more active in this area with Scout Troops and Boys' Clubs taking the lead. The Fladbury Canoe Club has been National Marathon and Sprint Club Champions. In the vicinity of this village large numbers of canoeists of all ages may be encountered training, especially on this reach upstream of Fladbury Lock. Canoes may also be encountered at Luddington and below Stratford weir. All other craft should keep a good look out for them, and show them due consideration.

Also, dragon boats may be encountered on the Pershore/Wyre reach and at Stratford upon Avon.

ROWING
Evesham Rowing Club based opposite town moorings at Evesham and Stratford upon Avon Rowing Club based opposite the RSC are the only rowing clubs on the Avon Navigation. Oarsmen may be encountered anywhere on these reaches. When passing them speed should be greatly reduced to ELIMINATE ALL WASH. At Stratford be aware of the possibility of large numbers of hired small boats on the river.

FISHING

The river provides good coarse fishing for bream, roach, perch, eels etc. A valid Environment Agency rod licence is required. Some fishing may be available at Luddington and enquiries may be made by telephoning the Trust's office. However, the majority of the rights from the banks are in the hands of private clubs and the Birmingham Anglers Association. Permits to fish these waters may be obtained from most tackle dealers.

Fishing is not permitted from boats moored (i) on the Workman Gardens, Evesham (ii) on Gasworks Wharf, Evesham (iii) on any Avon Navigation Trust mooring, and (iv) in the navigable channel. Also it is not allowed from weirs, locks and their landing stages, sluices, slipways or bridges.

SUPPLIES AND SERVICES

1.	GENERAL SERVICES and SUPPLIES at points shown in the table on page 55.

2.	MAINS WATER SUPPLY at Avon Lock, Tewkesbury, Evesham Lock and Evesham Town Moorings, Offenham Lock, Luddington, Bidford, Stratford Marina and the Old Bathing Place. Also at sanitary stations.

3.	SANITARY STATIONS and PUMP OUTS:
	See maps in book which are correct at the time of printing. The future of these sites is subject to revision and latest information may be obtained from the Registered Office or the residentially manned locks at Evesham and Tewkesbury.

4.	REFUSE DISPOSAL: Tewkesbury Town Moorings, Eckington Wharf, Pershore Recreation Ground (by swimming pool), Evesham Town Moorings, Offenham Lock, Luddington Lock.

5.	PUBLIC SWIMMING BATHS at Tewkesbury, Pershore, Evesham and Stratford upon Avon.

6.	FUEL (PETROL, DIESEL or GAS OIL) riverside supplies at:

Tewkesbury	Tewkesbury Marina
Evesham	Sankey Marine
Evesham	Evesham Marina
Stratford upon Avon	Stratford Marina

7.	HOSPITALS at Stratford upon Avon, Evesham, Pershore and Tewkesbury.

Tewkesbury, with King John's Bridge in the background

ADJOINING NAVIGATIONS

The Severn Waterway

The Navigation Authority for the Severn, and Gloucester - Sharpness Ship Canal, as for most of the country's nationalised waterways, is British Waterways.

Downstream the Severn leads through Gloucester Docks and the Ship Canal to Sharpness Docks and the sea. Upstream it leads to Worcester and Stourport where, at both places, are connecting locks with the main canal system.

Further information is available from British Waterways, Gloucester (01452 318000).

The Stratford-upon-Avon Canal
(Southern Section)

Having been restored under the auspices of the National Trust, this navigation is now owned and managed by British Waterways but, unlike the Avon river navigation, has "narrow" locks which will not accommodate craft of dimensions exceeding 71 ft 8 in x 7 ft x 3 ft/21.8 m x 2.1 m x 0.9 m.

It joins the Avon Navigation through the canal basin at Stratford-upon-Avon, ascends by thirty six locks in 13 miles/21 km to connect with the rest of the canal system at Lapworth.

The Stratford and Warwick Waterways Trust
Higher Avon Navigation

The Higher Avon is the section of the river between Alveston and Warwick where it is crossed by the Grand Union Canal. At present this section, which includes several weirs, is not continuously navigable. In 2006 a new charitable company, The Stratford and Warwick Waterways Trust Ltd, was formed with the object of restoring the Avon Navigation to the Grand Union Canal at Warwick. Membership details may be obtained from the Secretary at The Cottage Mill Lane Barford Warwick CV35 8EJ Telephone: 01926 624028   Website: www.swwaterway.co.uk

Environment Agency

The Environment Agency is the authority responsible for land drainage, flood control, fisheries, pollution control and water abstraction on the river. The Avon Navigation Trust is the authority responsible for locks and other navigational installations. Much of the work of the two bodies is complementary and there is a very close working relationship between them.

Avon Navigation Trust greatly appreciates the close liaison it enjoys with the Environment Agency and which it had with its predecessors and the help given by their respective officers and members over the years.

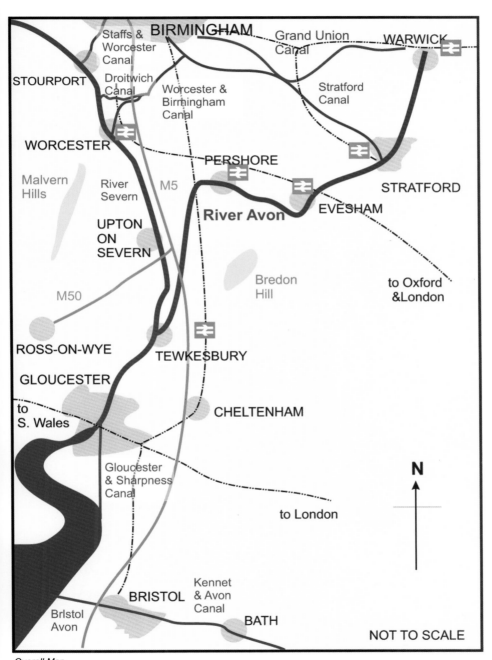

Overall Map

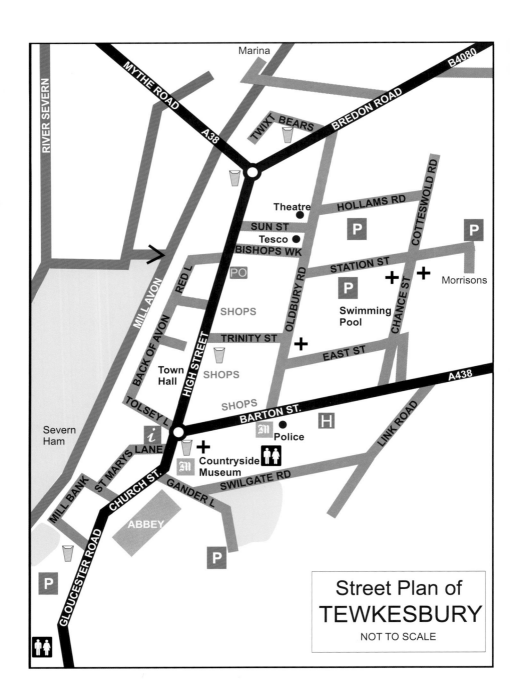

Street Plan of
TEWKESBURY
NOT TO SCALE

VISITORS GUIDE and NAVIGATION NOTES

In the following guide to the river and places of interest, the route taken is upstream from Tewkesbury and references to left and right are as they would be to anyone travelling upriver and, obviously, must be reversed when coming downstream. The left-hand column contains items of interest to the visitor to the Avon Valley. The right hand column is devoted to navigational notes. While it is hoped that this book will provide most of the information needed by anyone to enjoy their holiday on the Avon, it is recommended that the 1:50,000 Ordnance Survey Landranger Series Sheets 150 (Worcester and the Malverns) and 151 (Stratford upon Avon) or 1:25,000 Explorer 190 (Malvern Hills and Bredon Hill) and 205 (Stratford upon Avon and Bredon) should be obtained as they cover all of the river between Stratford and Tewkesbury. Grid references in these notes will help in the location of places on these maps.

Visitors Guide
Tewkesbury to Bredon/ Bredon to Strensham

Apart from the shopping facilities it offers, **TEWKESBURY** has a main street with varied architecture and some historic inns. The abbey, now used as a parish church, has an 11th century tower and much internal work of architectural and historic interest. There was a small church on the site in the 7th century and a monastery founded there in the 9th century. Tewkesbury is the town featured in "John Halifax, Gentleman" and Abel Fletcher's mill (Abbey Mill) still remains, although converted to residential use. Tewkesbury was also noted for its boat builders who produced sea-going motor yachts.

The downstream end of Avon lock was substantially rebuilt and the lock working mechanised in 1976. The chamber was refurbished, new bottom gates fitted and other improvements carried out in 1989 and 1990.

ACTUAL DIMENSIONS, ABOVE NORMAL SUMMER RETENTION LEVEL, KING JOHN'S BRIDGE, TEWKESBURY

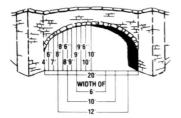

Navigation Notes
Passage between River Severn and Avon Lock (See map on page 24)

The Avon Navigation commences at the confluence with the Severn downstream of Avon Lock. At this point a Trust licence is required, obtainable from the Lock Keeper.

The junction is 600 yards/550 m downstream of Mythe Bridge, Tewkesbury, and is easy to miss. There is a very shallow spit projecting out into the river at this point which must be given a wide berth. This entails, when passaging downstream on the Severn, passing the actual junction before making the turn into the Avon. Similarly, when leaving the Avon do not turn upstream on the Severn until the Mythe Bridge is visible in full.

All craft with VHF radio about to navigate the River Avon between the confluence with the River Severn and Quay Pit, Avon Lock, the Old Avon or Stanchard Pit, in either direction should:

(i) Keep radio watch on Channel 16 for 10 minutes before entering this section and during passage
(ii) Call "Any craft on passage on the Avon Navigation between the Severn and Tewkesbury" and switch to an alternative channel to discuss intentions.

Navigators are further advised:
(i) Some helmsmen traversing this section of the Navigation may be inexperienced holiday makers and do not carry VHF
(ii) Because of the potential danger to smaller craft, two very large vessels should not transit this section in opposite directions at the same time.

Craft should also take care to avoid the mudbank which extends from the bank opposite Healing's Mill by steering a course close to the Town Quay downstream of the mill.

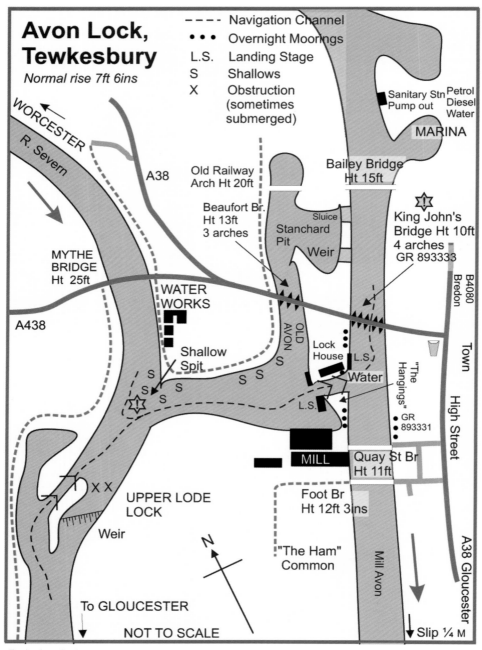

Avon Lock, Tewkesbury

Normal rise 7ft 6ins

- - - - Navigation Channel
- • • • Overnight Moorings
- L.S. Landing Stage
- S Shallows
- X Obstruction (sometimes submerged)

WORCESTER

R. Severn

A38

Old Railway Arch Ht 20ft

Beaufort Br. Ht 13ft 3 arches

Stanchard Pit

Sluice

Weir

MYTHE BRIDGE Ht 25ft

A438

WATER WORKS

Shallow Spit

OLD AVON

S S S S S

S S S S

Sanitary Stn Pump out

Petrol Diesel Water

MARINA

Bailey Bridge Ht 15ft

King John's Bridge Ht 10ft 4 arches GR 893333

B4080 Bredon

Lock House

L.S.

Water

"The Hangings"

L.S.

GR 893331

Town

High Street

UPPER LODE LOCK

X X

Weir

MILL

Quay St Br Ht 11ft

Foot Br Ht 12ft 3ins

"The Ham" Common

N

Mill Avon

A38 Gloucester

To GLOUCESTER

NOT TO SCALE

Slip ¼ M

Tewkesbury Lock

Visitors Guide

In the open reaches between Tewkesbury and Strensham lock, the water is used by several dinghy sailing clubs and the clubhouses of Tewkesbury Cruising & Sailing Club and the Severn Sailing Club are prominent. (The Avon Sailing Club is on the Severn!)

The first landmark upriver of Tewkesbury is TWYNING FLEET INN on the left. It is a short distance up the lane beside the inn to the village of Twyning Green, with a post office. The lane from the disused ferry landing on the opposite bank only leads to the Tewkesbury/Bredon road.

In the village of **BREDON** there are a few shops and a post office, an obelisk milestone and some timbered houses. A large barn can be seen as Bredon is approached by river. This dates from the 14th century and is owned by the National Trust, who permit visiting free during daylight. The church with a prominent spire dates, in part, from the 12th century.

BREDON HILL seems to be with you for many miles. It is 980 ft/300 m high and is an outlier of the Cotswolds with the remains of an Iron Age fort at the top. There are tracks up Bredon Hill from several points. The top is about 4 miles/6.4 km from Bredon village or about half this by a steeper climb from Great Comberton.

Strensham Lock

Navigation Notes

Downstream at Avon Lock, Tewkesbury, the old Avon channel continues straight on past the lock, through Beaufort Bridge, clearance 13 ft/ 3.9 m, leading to a mooring basin where overnight mooring can generally be arranged particularly for vessels which are too large to use the lock. At the lock entrance a green light denotes the lock all clear for entry, a red light denotes entrance foul and craft should stand off or moor to a lock landing stage, if room available. No lights indicate that either the lock is set for manual operation by boat crews or closed if after hours unless a late or early locking has been previously booked.

The upstream gates which incorporate a footbridge must be left closed and the chain which prevents them swinging open replaced when leaving the lock unattended.

By the top gate on the opposite side to the house there is a height gauge showing the air draught or clearance under the centre of the navigation arch of King John's Bridge with the river level as it is when leaving the lock.

Tewkesbury to Bredon (See map on page 26)

After locking through Avon Lock, where there is a resident lock keeper and mains water (telephone 01684 292129) visitors' moorings are about 50 yards downstream by Healings Mill and defined by notice boards and also alongside the wall of Red Lane on the east or opposite bank. Further information should be obtained from the lock keeper. When leaving the lock proceeding upstream or downstream, great care should be exercised as, at both ends, the lock joins almost at right angles the busy upper and lower reaches along which passes considerable traffic. This is particularly important when proceeding downstream as visibility up the old Avon to the right is restricted by the depth of the chamber.

All services are available within easy walking distance.

Proceeding upstream, craft need to pass under King John's Bridge (grid ref 893332) where visibility is restricted, therefore make sound signal (4 second blast) and use extreme caution and minimum speed. There is a jetty for a sanitary station on the right hand bank, in front of Tewkesbury Marine Dock Office, upstream of the refuelling pontoon. Water is available and a charge is made for pump-out facilities. There follows a broad reach of the river very suitable for sailing although now spanned just before Bredon by the M5 motorway bridge which gives a clearance of 25 ft/7.6 m at normal summer level. Moorings can be taken en route at Twyning Fleet (grid ref 905366).

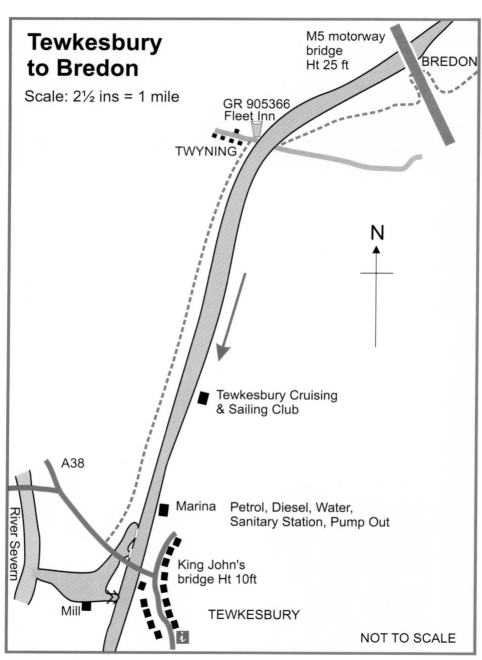

Tewkesbury to Bredon

Scale: 2½ ins = 1 mile

M5 motorway bridge Ht 25 ft

BREDON

GR 905366 Fleet Inn

TWYNING

N

Tewkesbury Cruising & Sailing Club

A38

River Severn

Marina — Petrol, Diesel, Water, Sanitary Station, Pump Out

King John's bridge Ht 10ft

Mill

TEWKESBURY

NOT TO SCALE

Tewkesbury to Bredon

Birlingham Village Church

Navigation Notes

Bredon to Strensham Lock
(See map on page 28)

The old wharf at Bredon Dock is now fenced off from the river and is no longer available for mooring although the installation of floating pontoons is being investigated.

Continuing upstream the Coventry Waterworks pipe bridge gives a clearance of 23 ft/7 m and shortly afterwards the entrance to STRENSHAM LOCK can be seen (grid ref 915404).

The Old Mill House has been reconditioned and is now a private residence. From the lock a road runs up to Eckington village and shops etc, and for a short duration overnight mooring may be available. There is a sanitary station and water point on the left bank immediately following the first right hand turn after the lock.

Leaving Strensham Lock

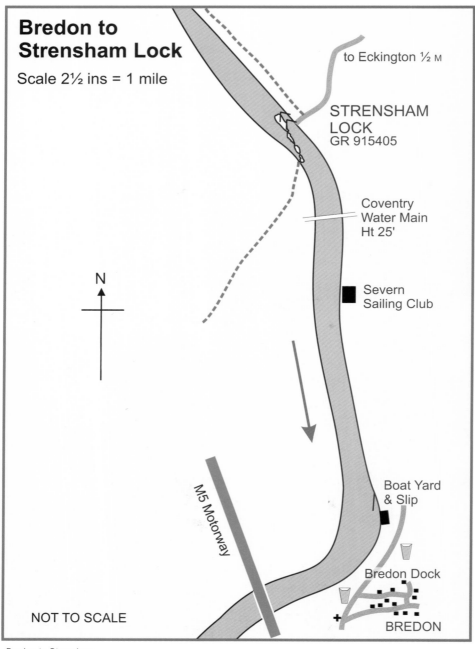

Bredon to Strensham Lock

Scale 2½ ins = 1 mile

to Eckington ½ M

STRENSHAM
LOCK
GR 915405

Coventry
Water Main
Ht 25'

N

Severn
Sailing Club

M5 Motorway

Boat Yard
& Slip

Bredon Dock

BREDON

NOT TO SCALE

Bredon to Strensham

Strensham Lock

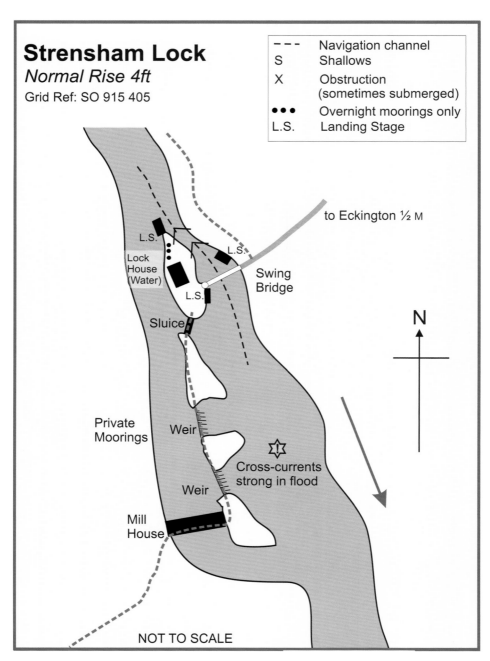

Strensham Lock
Normal Rise 4ft
Grid Ref: SO 915 405

- - -	Navigation channel
S	Shallows
X	Obstruction (sometimes submerged)
●●●	Overnight moorings only
L.S.	Landing Stage

to Eckington ½ M

L.S.

L.S.

Lock House (Water)

Swing Bridge

L.S.

N

Sluice

Private Moorings

Weir

Cross-currents strong in flood

Weir

Mill House

NOT TO SCALE

Strensham Lock

Visitors Guide

Strensham Lock to Nafford Lock

The lock and its house are historically interesting as the Trust brought the lock back from near dereliction in 1950/1 as one of its early projects, and restored the Old Eckington Mill House and made it habitable in 1952, but more extensive work was required in 1970/1. The lock was mechanised in 1975 but has now reverted to manual operation. The upstream gates were replaced in 1992 and the downstream in 2002.

The lock is named after the hamlet of STRENSHAM, where a church can be seen on the hill on the left bank upriver of the lock. This little church (keyholder nearby in village) has a painted gallery, stained glass and 16th century pews, and there are some nearby 17th century almshouses. All of this once quiet backwater is now within a short distance of a service area on the M5 motorway.

Roman remains were discovered recently in the village of Eckington. It has shops for provisioning, a church which dates in part from the 12th century, a cookery school and two pubs. There is a 3.5 mile / 7km walk based on Eckington Wharf.

The Clubhouse of the Arden Sailing Club, which is associated with Malvern College, is passed on the left just before the railway bridge.

Defford Rail Bridge

Navigation Notes

Strensham Lock to Nafford Lock
(See map on page 32)

From Strensham the river winds its way under Defford Railway bridge (grid ref 917425) clearance 25 ft/7.6 m to Eckington Bridge (grid ref 922422) about two miles/3.2 km upstream where, at low summer level, the clearance is 10 ft 6 in/3.2 m at the centre of the arch (see diagram).

ACTUAL DIMENSIONS, ABOVE NORMAL SUMMER RETENTION LEVEL, ECKINGTON BRIDGE

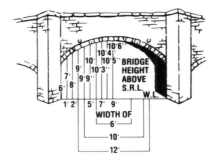

SEE ADDITIONAL IMPORTANT NOTES ON NAVIGATING ECKINGTON BRIDGE AT TIMES OF "FRESHWATER" on page 34.

Here the mooring for visitors can be taken immediately upstream of the bridge (on the RIGHT HAND BANK facing upstream ONLY) at Eckington Wharf. Mooring on the left hand bank immediately upstream is very dangerous and this area must be avoided.

Again, from this point a visit can be paid to Eckington village which has all the usual amenities.

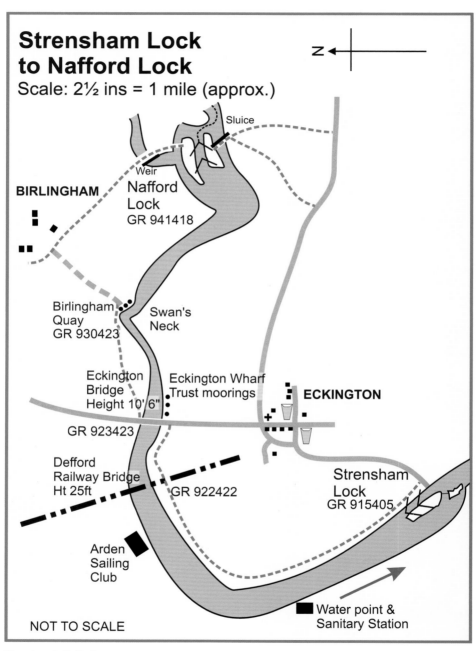

Strensham Lock to Nafford Lock

Scale: 2½ ins = 1 mile (approx.)

Z

Sluice

Weir

BIRLINGHAM

Nafford Lock
GR 941418

Birlingham Quay
GR 930423

Swan's Neck

Eckington Bridge
Height 10' 6"

GR 923423

Eckington Wharf
Trust moorings

ECKINGTON

Defford Railway Bridge
Ht 25ft

GR 922422

Strensham Lock
GR 915405

Arden Sailing Club

■ Water point & Sanitary Station

NOT TO SCALE

Strensham to Nafford

Visitors Guide

ECKINGTON BRIDGE with its irregular arches of different sizes has stood since the 16th century. While it may, at times, be a slight hazard to boating, it is a tribute to the masons of those days, who built a structure still in good condition over 400 years later.

The railway line through Eckington should be of interest to railway enthusiasts. It is almost straight for many miles and is the main line from Exeter to Newcastle-upon-Tyne.

BIRLINGHAM village is a short walk from the river, either from the Quay or from Nafford Lock. It is a typical example of many villages in this area - charming and quiet with an excellent pub.

Eckington Bridge viewed from

Below Nafford Lock, showing the sluices on the right

Navigating through Eckington Bridge and the old Pershore Great Bridge at time of "fresh" water

Only the largest arch in these ancient multi-arched bridges should be used for navigation.

Whilst not wishing to over-emphasise the danger which develops at these bridges at such times when the river has risen above normal level it is nevertheless necessary to indicate the danger that does exist.

Naturally, as a result of heavy rainfall over a long period the river will rise and the rate of flow increases. This in turn lessens headroom beneath the bridge, and develops turbulence in the area immediately downstream and upstream of the bridge piers.

IT IS ADVISABLE ON SUCH OCCASIONS TO WAIT A DAY OR TWO TO ALLOW THE RIVER TO FALL AND FOR BETTER NAVIGATION CONDITIONS. If navigation is attempted, then be sure to "square-up" to the centre arch so that the craft cannot be swept against the piers, or if travelling downstream, to be swept broadside across the bridge.

At all times, craft navigating upstream should give way to those travelling downstream. IF IN DOUBT, STOP, MOOR UP AND SEEK ADVICE.

Visitors Guide

From Birlingham Quay on the outside of the Swan's Neck Bend there is a pleasant walk to Birlingham village.

Also at **NAFFORD LOCK** the footpath which crosses by a bridge over the lock, leads to the left over a weir to Birlingham. To the right the footpath crosses the sluices and leads to a lane between Eckington and Great Comberton. Up the slope of Bredon Hill a private road leads to Woollas Hall (grid ref 947405). This is an Elizabethan manor house, with a three-story porch and some fine paintings and furniture.

The sluices alongside Nafford Lock and other similar works on the river are operated by the Environment Agency, which is responsible for drainage of the Avon and other tributaries of the River Severn. Although they are not concerned with navigation, much of their work is of benefit to boat users, and these are interesting examples of navigation and drainage authorities working in parallel.

The footbridge crossing Nafford Weir and the swing bridge across Nafford Lock are maintained by the Worcestershire County Council.

Nothing remains of the village of Nafford which was wiped out over 300 years ago by a landslide on Bredon Hill.

Navigation Notes

It is three quarters of a mile/1.2 km upstream of Eckington Bridge to the Swan's Neck Bend and Birlingham Quay (grid ref 930423). Here the river becomes narrow and circuitous, and craft have to negotiate this bend of 180 degrees, which calls for general caution, a good look out for craft approaching from the opposite direction and a considerable reduction in speed.

Similar bends occur between this point and NAFFORD LOCK (grid ref 940418). The navigation channel is in accordance with the plan on page 36 and the swing bridge MUST be opened before using this lock and closed prior to leaving.

After a lengthy period of wet weather, or because of continuous heavy rainfall, the river can rise above the normal level. This "fresh" (surplus water) is drawn off by the steel sluices in order to prevent flooding of the land. At such time, due to increased rate of river flow and suction from the sluice race it is dangerous to approach too closely to these sluices on their upstream (higher) level, especially to the one adjacent to Nafford Lock. When travelling downstream, craft should be steered to the island and kept moving forward towards the lock entrance.

Nafford Island is a bird sanctuary and mooring to or walking on this island is prohibited.

Eckington Bridge and Bredon Hill

Nafford Lock

Normal Rise 5ft 6ins

Grid Ref: SO 941 418

NOT TO SCALE

– – –	Navigation channel
S	Shallows
X	Obstruction (sometimes submerged)
●●●	Overnight moorings only
L.S.	Landing Stage

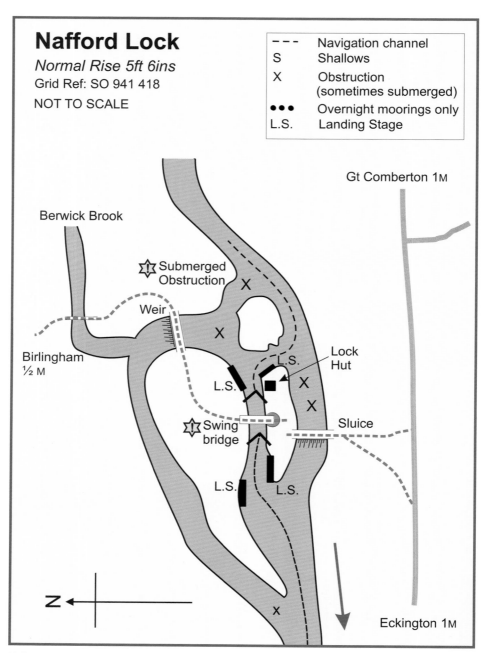

Gt Comberton 1ᴍ

Berwick Brook

Submerged Obstruction

Weir

Birlingham ½ M

Lock Hut

L.S.

L.S.

Swing bridge

Sluice

L.S.

L.S.

N

Eckington 1ᴍ

Nafford Lock

Visitors Guide

Nafford Lock to Pershore Lock

GREAT COMBERTON and nearby LITTLE COMBERTON are at the foot of the northern slopes of Bredon Hill. A path from Great Comberton leads up the hill. About 2 miles/3.2 km further east around the foot of the hill the village of ELMLEY CASTLE is noted for its half timbered houses.

The shoal before the boatyard downstream of the Pershore Bridges is all the evidence that is left of the Pershore Watergate, one of the last of the old-style staunches (sometimes called Flash Locks or Wyres) in regular use anywhere, which was removed by the Trust as recently as 1956. The single gate here was closed to hold back and raise the water to enable a barge to float in sufficient depth to reach Pershore Mill. This meant that passage of the watergate either way might mean a wait of several hours, using sluices to bring the level the same both sides and allow the gate to be opened.

Up to here the country adjoining the river has been mainly pleasantly rural and given over to mixed farming, with crops, cattle and sheep. From the vicinity of Pershore, use of the land changes to more fruit growing and market gardening.

Dinghes from Arden Sailing Club

Navigation Notes

Nafford Lock to Pershore Lock
(See map on page 38)
About half a mile/ 0.8 km upstream of Nafford, on the right-hand bank facing upstream, is an overnight mooring at Comberton Quay, from where the village of Great Comberton is worth a visit. On the opposite bank 1¾ miles/2.8 km further on, where the road runs near to the river, and situated between two lengths of bank in use as permanent moorings, is Defford Road Wharf - another overnight site (grid ref 931445). Some four miles/6.4 km upstream of Nafford before reaching Pershore, and immediately after negotiating the left hand bend from which a boatyard is visible ahead on the right hand bank, care should be taken to keep to the left of the centre of the river to avoid a shoal.

Following or during periods of heavy or prolonged rainfall, the Flood Control Sluices at Pershore may be open causing a very strong current and dangerous eddies in the vicinity of both Pershore Bridges. Under these conditions vessels travelling upstream should stop downstream of Pershore New Bridge and vessels travelling downstream should not proceed beyond Pershore Lock. **WHEN IN DOUBT, STOP AND SEEK ADVICE.** See additional important notes on navigating the old Pershore Great Bridge at times of "fresh" water on page 34.

Immediately before the Pershore Bridges on the right hand bank are the Pershore Bridge Picnic Place moorings with access over the New Bridge to the town. Having passed under the New Bridge and the old Pershore Great Bridge (grid ref 952451) which give 13 ft 6 in/3.9 m and 12 ft/3.6 m clearance respectively, craft should keep to the centre of the narrow cutting downstream of PERSHORE LOCK (grid ref 952456), proceeding very slowly.

There is a very limited overnight mooring downstream of the lock landing stage on the right hand bank, but on no account must there be any breasting up or encroachment beyond the indicated limits onto the lock stage. There is no access to the town.

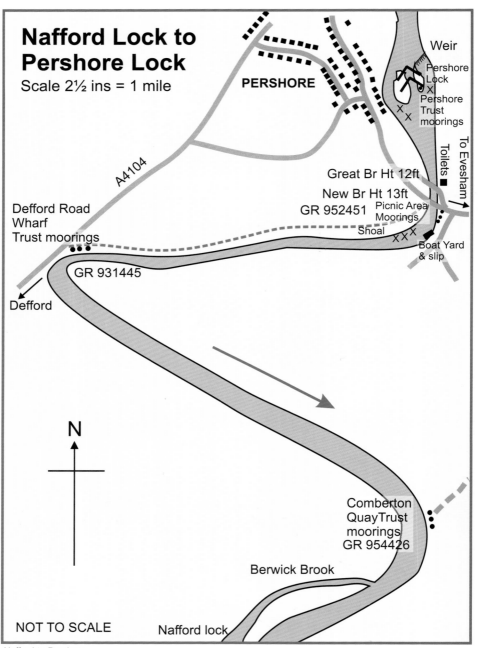

Nafford Lock to Pershore Lock

Scale 2½ ins = 1 mile

PERSHORE

Weir

Pershore Lock

X Pershore Trust moorings

To Evesham

Toilets

A4104

Great Br Ht 12ft

New Br Ht 13ft

GR 952451

Picnic Area Moorings

Shoal

Boat Yard & slip

Defford Road Wharf Trust moorings

GR 931445

Defford

N

Comberton QuayTrust moorings GR 954426

Berwick Brook

NOT TO SCALE

Nafford lock

Nafford to Pershore

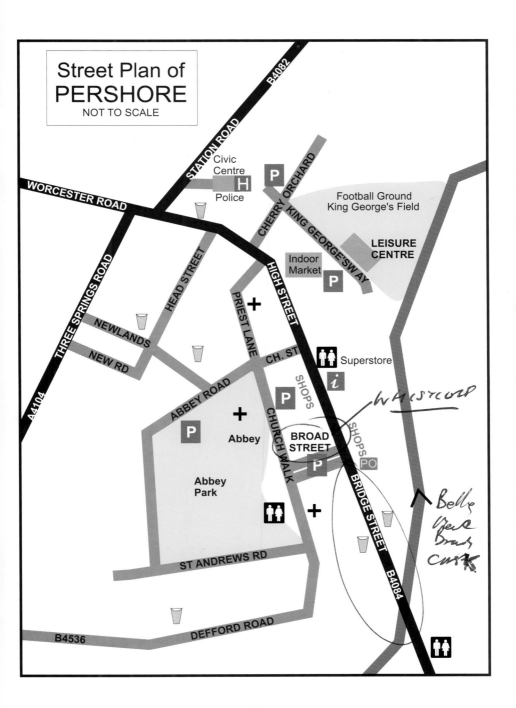

Street Plan of **PERSHORE**
NOT TO SCALE

39

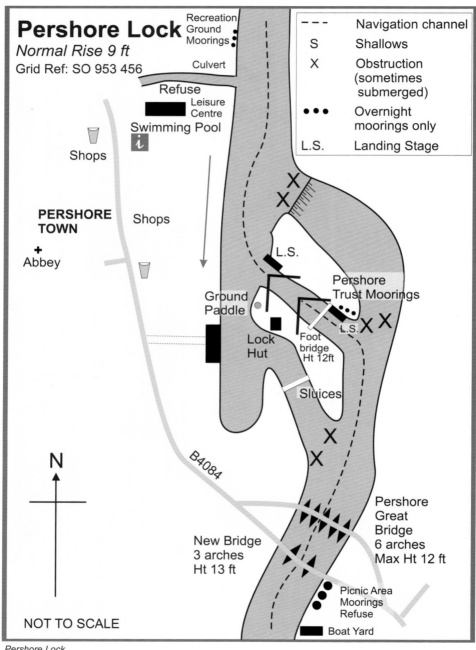

Pershore Lock

Visitors Guide

Pershore Lock to Cropthorne Heath

PERSHORE is a busy small town in some ways similar to Tewkesbury, with mixed architecture, including some Georgian houses with coach entrances and gardens to the river along the main street and a parish church which was once an abbey. It claims to have the finest Georgian Street in England. This area is near the downriver end of the fruit growing country known as the "Vale of Evesham". The fruit and vegetable market at Pershore was the first co-operative effort of its type, when it was started in 1909. It has now moved to a business park outside the town.

Also there is an excellent retail market held on Wednesdays, Thursdays, Fridays and Saturdays.

The main bridge which carries the Evesham/Worcester road through the town and which was the first reinforced concrete bridge to be built in Worcestershire, in 1928, is beside an old bridge, Pershore Great Bridge, of similar age to Eckington Bridge, but which no longer has to stand up to the traffic.

PERSHORE ABBEY suffered more than Tewkesbury Abbey. Part of the pre-10th century abbey was destroyed in the dissolution, but the remaining nave and central tower are used as a parish church. Here the most important saint venerated is the little-known St Edburga. Her story can be learned by a visit to the church. Another adjoining church was built as a result of the resentment of the monks when abbey land was taken from them in the 11th century.

Navigation Notes

Pershore Lock to Cropthorne Heath

(See map page 42)

There is a fixed footbridge across the tail of the lock giving the air draught or clearance of 11'6" at normal summer retention level but care should be exercised as operation of the adjacent Environment Agency sluices can affect the river level of the section between the Lock and Pershore Great Bridge immediately down stream. Refer to the clearance gauge on the lock wall adjacent to the bottom gates.

Special circumstances exist at Pershore Lock in that it has a ground paddle situated on the hut (town) side as well as two top gate paddles.

When filling the chamber to lock up, it is essential that the ground paddle be drawn first, after ensuring that the boat is secure with lines ashore fore and aft, these being adjusted as the water rises. When the top gate paddles are submerged, these may then be raised.

When emptying the chamber to lock down, check that the ground paddle is fully closed as well as those on the top gates.

Moorings for Pershore town, with quick and direct access to the main street, PO and shops, can be found at the recreation ground, King George's Field, on the reach above Pershore Lock. This is the meadow on the left hand bank (facing upstream) after passing all the private gardens and the Angel Hotel moorings, all of which come to the water's edge. The mooring area is clearly defined by blue mooring posts and notices placed at the bank side.

The reach above Pershore Lock is the shortest on the navigation, being just over one mile/1.6 km before WYRE LOCK (grid ref 959469) comes into sight.

Do not approach the weir tails here as heavy reinforcing stone has been deposited there.

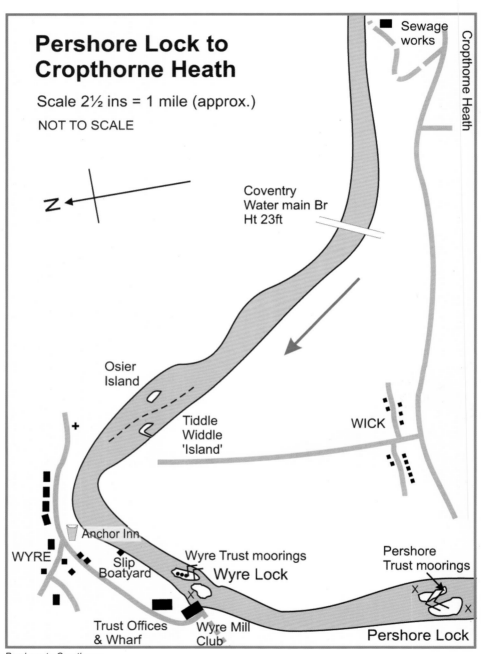

Pershore Lock to Cropthorne Heath

Scale 2½ ins = 1 mile (approx.)

NOT TO SCALE

Cropthorne Heath

Sewage works

Coventry Water main Br Ht 23ft

Z

Osier Island

Tiddle Widdle 'Island'

WICK

+

Anchor Inn

WYRE

Slip Boatyard

Wyre Trust moorings

Wyre Lock

Pershore Trust moorings

Trust Offices & Wharf

Wyre Mill Club

Pershore Lock

Pershore to Cropthorne

42

Visitors Guide

Adjacent to Wyre Lock stands Wyre Mill Club, an old gristmill that was converted by enthusiastic supporters of The Lower Avon Navigation Trust into a Social Club and is now owned by the Club's members. This property is set aside for the exclusive use of the Club's members, but in an emergency, telephone calls may be made upon application to the Club Manager.

Owners of craft who are members of the Avon Navigation Trust and are visiting the River Avon for a short period only, also Avon Navigation Trust members who are operating a hire craft on the waterway, will be very welcome as temporary members of Wyre Mill Club, subject to mooring being available and to the usual rules for Club premises and especially the rule which prescribes that advantage cannot be taken of the licensed portion of the premises until 48 hours after becoming a member. In any case, prior notice is required.

In the reach upstream of Wyre Lock the boatman is at last beginning to lose sight of Bredon Hill. The adjoining low-lying water meadows are subject to flooding, so there are no villages or nearby roads once slightly elevated Wyre Piddle has been passed, until Jubilee Bridge is reached.

Navigation Notes

As well as the Trust's Office, its maintenance wharf is situated alongside the mill on the upper reach but is reserved for working craft, some of which may be seen in the vicinity, and is NOT available for overnight or other pleasure craft mooring.

Wyre Lock is diamond shaped and is of uniform depth. The lock was refurbished in the winter 1994/95 retaining the same historic shape.

On the left, immediately on leaving the upstream lock channel, there is an overnight mooring on the lock island but there is no land access to the village. On the opposite bank is a slipway.

Continuing upstream, the village of Wyre Piddle (grid ref 966474) is approached. It stands high up on the left bank and many of the gardens of private houses, together with the land of the village inn, The Anchor, reach right down to the water's edge. At present there is no known public landing place, but the inn provides a landing stage for the benefit of its customers.
Discussions are taking place regarding the installation of overnight moorings downstream of the village.

The next navigational landmark is the Coventry water main bridge (clearance 23 ft/7 m) but care should be exercised to hold as far as practicable to the centre or outside of the various bends, shoals extending in some cases up to one-third of the width of the river from the inside bank.

A barge negotiates Pershore Great Bridge

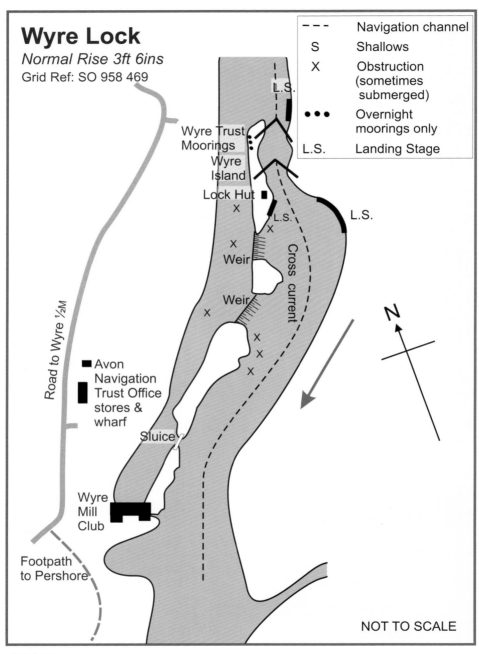

Wyre Lock
Normal Rise 3ft 6ins
Grid Ref: SO 958 469

	Navigation channel
S	Shallows
X	Obstruction (sometimes submerged)
•••	Overnight moorings only
L.S.	Landing Stage

L.S.

Wyre Trust Moorings

Wyre Island

Lock Hut ■

X

X   L.S.

X

X

Weir

X   Weir

X

X

X

X

Cross current

L.S.

N

Road to Wyre ½M

■ Avon
Navigation
Trust Office
stores &
wharf

Sluice

Wyre
Mill
Club

Footpath
to Pershore

NOT TO SCALE

Wyre Lock

Visitors Guide

Cropthorne Heath to Chadbury

JUBILEE BRIDGE carries a local road between Fladbury and Cropthorne villages. About 100 yards/90 m downstream is all that now remains of the old flash lock - some brickwork and masonry on both banks.

This old flash lock, Cropthorne Watergate, was another staunch similar to that below Pershore, but it fell out of use earlier and was a hazard to navigation. It was removed by the Trust in 1961. At the same time the channel was dredged up to Fladbury Lock and the lock deepened. A stone deflector wall was placed between the weir and the lock entrance, and a piled landing stage provided. At the time, this project was the most expensive and cost an overall sum of £20,000 to complete.

Fladbury Lock was refurbished in 2008.

In order to visit the two villages of Fladbury and Cropthorne, craft owners should moor in the vicinity of the Jubilee Bridge. Here, standing on the bridge and facing upstream, to the right lie the roads to Cropthorne and Charlton, while to the left is a short walk to the village of Fladbury. From Fladbury Lock and Weir there is a fine view of the two mills there and the river reach above the lock.

The mill between **FLADBURY LOCK** and Fladbury Weir is rather unexpectedly called Cropthorne Mill, while Fladbury Mill is on the bank at the end of the weir. Cropthorne Mill has long been a residence of the Barrow family of Birmingham (long-standing supporters of the Trust.) Fladbury church is on the left bank just above the lock.

Navigation Notes

Cropthorne Heath to Chadbury
(See map on page 46)

We next come to Jubilee Bridge (grid ref 000456) clearance 14 ft/4.2m.

IT IS ESSENTIAL that great care should be taken at this part of the navigation to comply in every way with the instructions given - see map on page 48. The channel, for 200 yards/180 m below Jubilee Bridge has been dredged from the Fladbury (left hand) bank and is only 60 ft/18 m wide. The map clearly marks the position of underwater obstructions.

Also on the map on page 48 are instructions relating to the approach to FLADBURY LOCK where the clearance under the footbridge at the tail of the lock is 11 ft 6 in/3.5 m. There are no particular hazards in the operation of this lock, except that it tapers slightly inwards towards the bottom of the chamber and it is therefore possible for two boats, whose total beam makes it a tight fit in the lock when full, to be crushed when locking down. When travelling downstream the lock entrance is not very obvious at a distance. Keep a good look out for the ferry wires to one side of the lock.

Soon after leaving the lock you will pass under the railway bridge clearance 16 ft/4.8 m, which carries the main line from Worcester to London across the river.

The golf course of Evesham Golf Club is passed, also on the left, adjoining Craycombe Hill.

Between Craycombe and Chadbury the river makes some big loops, running between lush meadows with, on the left, another overnight mooring at Craycombe Turn. The Wood Norton hills are on the Fladbury side and, beyond the opposite bank, Bredon Hill or the upper part of it is always on the horizon.

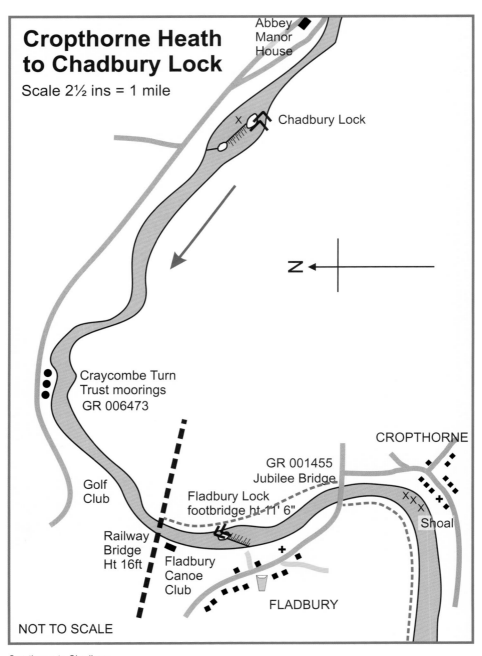

Cropthorne Heath to Chadbury Lock

Scale 2½ ins = 1 mile

Abbey Manor House

Chadbury Lock

Z ←

Craycombe Turn
Trust moorings
GR 006473

CROPTHORNE

GR 001455
Jubilee Bridge

Golf
Club

Fladbury Lock
footbridge ht 11' 6"

X X X

Shoal

Railway
Bridge
Ht 16ft

Fladbury
Canoe
Club

FLADBURY

NOT TO SCALE

Cropthorne to Chadbury

Visitors Guide

FLADBURY is notable in the history of the river as the home of William Sandys, who first started to make the river navigable in 1636. About 1 mile/1.6 km upriver on the left bank, but not visible from the river, is Craycombe House. This was built by George Perrott, who purchased the Navigation of the Lower Avon towards the end of the 18th century and in whose family it remained until 1924. Craycombe House was also the home of the writer Francis Brett Young for a few years.

Both Fladbury and Cropthorne are picturesque villages with many examples of the local black and white half timbered houses, set in lovely surroundings. Cropthorne, in particular, is a tourist attraction. The road is on the blossom route marked for cyclists and motorists in the Spring. Orchards and gardens here and in the next few miles are worth visiting and plenty of produce is available from roadside stalls.

At the opposite end of the weir from Chadbury Mill is **CHADBURY LOCK**. Its complete rebuilding was the first major task of the Trust, in 1952/3, being largely carried out by Royal Engineers. It was the first civilian aid project carried out by the armed forces.

Without this work which prevented the complete collapse of the old structure and the river above, Evesham would have been left with a shallow, muddy stream.

Above the left bank, amidst woods and parkland, is Wood Norton, for some time a hotel and conference centre, but once the seat of the Duke of Orleans, pretender to the throne of France, and also used by King Manuel when he was deposed from the throne of Portugal in 1910. In 1907 the sister of the Duke of Orleans, Princess Louise of France, was married here to Prince Charles of Bourbon.

Navigation Notes

Soon we come to Chadbury Mill, and a little later, CHADBURY LOCK (grid ref 025460). From Chadbury there is a good straight stretch practically up to the railway bridge near Evesham railway station. On the left the land rises from the river, which runs close to a high road beyond which are the woodlands of the old Abbey Manor estate.

When travelling downstream the lock entrance is concealed by trees until almost opposite. The crest of Chadbury Weir is unmarked and invisible. Slow speed and great caution are advised.

Descending Fladbury Lock

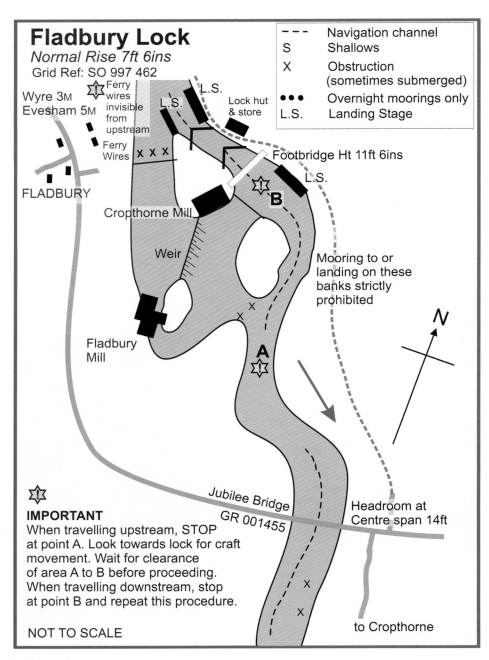

Fladbury Lock
Normal Rise 7ft 6ins
Grid Ref: SO 997 462

Wyre 3M
Evesham 5M

Ferry wires invisible from upstream

Ferry Wires

FLADBURY

L.S.

L.S.

L.S.

Lock hut & store

Cropthorne Mill

Weir

Fladbury Mill

X X X

Footbridge Ht 11ft 6ins

L.S.

B

Mooring to or landing on these banks strictly prohibited

A

N

	Navigation channel
– – –	Navigation channel
S	Shallows
X	Obstruction (sometimes submerged)
●●●	Overnight moorings only
L.S.	Landing Stage

Jubilee Bridge
GR 001455

Headroom at Centre span 14ft

to Cropthorne

IMPORTANT
When travelling upstream, STOP at point A. Look towards lock for craft movement. Wait for clearance of area A to B before proceeding. When travelling downstream, stop at point B and repeat this procedure.

NOT TO SCALE

Fladbury Lock

Below Fladbury Lock

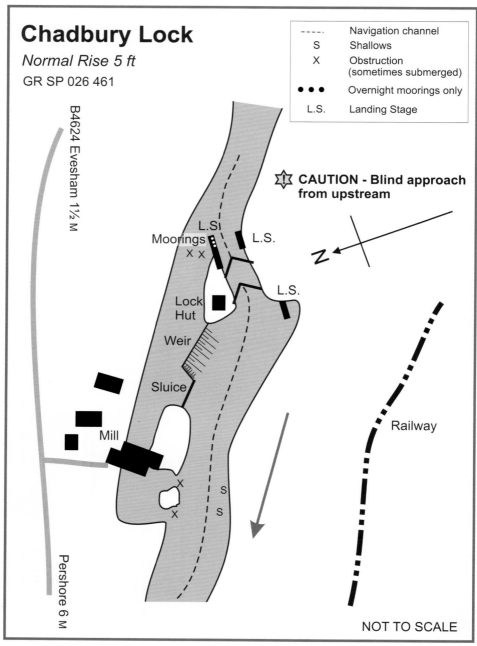

Chadbury Lock

Normal Rise 5 ft

GR SP 026 461

----.	Navigation channel
S	Shallows
X	Obstruction (sometimes submerged)
●●●	Overnight moorings only
L.S.	Landing Stage

B4624 Evesham 1½ M

⚠ **CAUTION - Blind approach from upstream**

N

L.S.
Moorings
X X
L.S.

L.S.

Lock Hut

Weir

Sluice

Mill

X
X

S
S

Railway

NOT TO SCALE

Pershore 6 M

Chadbury Lock

Visitors Guide

Chadbury to Offenham

About 1 mile/1.6 km above Chadbury Lock at the end of the straight stretch, in the grounds of **ABBEY MANOR** on the left, is an obelisk marking the site of the Battle of Evesham on 4 August 1265, at which Simon de Montfort, the Earl of Leicester was killed. Another memorial of the same event is Leicester Tower built about 1840 and visible in the woodland.

Upstream of the railway bridge carrying the main Worcester-London line, on the right hand bank are the terraces of **CLARK'S HILL** dating from the days when the monks of Evesham Abbey grew vines here.

Today the town of Evesham includes the former parishes of Bengeworth and Great and Little Hampton on the opposite bank of the river.

Above Abbey Park, Evesham, may be seen the spires of All Saints and St Lawrence's Churches, as well as the famous Bell Tower, all within the same churchyard. Very little is left of the huge Abbey Church. Evesham grew up around this monastery, founded in 702, but this was destroyed by Henry VIII in 1539. There is a 14th century stone and wood framed building called the Almonry, on the site of the Benedictine Abbey. This is open to the public most afternoons at a fee, and houses one of the best local museums in the county.

The town contains many timber framed buildings of historic interest. Like nearby Stratford (15 miles/24 km) many of the buildings date from Tudor days. Younger members of the crew may be interested in the jaw bones of a whale forming an arch in the Workman Gardens.

Navigation Notes

Chadbury to Offenham
(See map on page 52)

Having passed under the railway bridge (grid ref 032446) clearance 25 ft/7.6 m there is a water point and sanitary station on the right bank at Hampton Park. We then begin to negotiate the huge loop which makes the old town of Evesham a peninsula.

Proceeding, we soon come to the picturesque Hampton Ferry (grid ref 029436). The ferry is rope-operated and extreme caution is necessary to avoid fouling the rope. **THREE BLASTS ON THE HOOTER** is the accepted signal for the ferryman to lower the rope to permit the passage of boats. Power craft should proceed slowly past the mooring (4 mph max) to the rope site and cross in neutral so that the rope will not be sucked into the propeller. Opposite the Ferry House is the licensed restaurant where arrangements to moor should be made with the ferryman.

At a point approximately 300 yards/275 m upstream of the ferry there is a bad shoal of heavy masonry protruding about 10 yards/9.2 m from the right hand bank (facing upstream). This extends for almost 150 yards/140 m, and is identified by a line of withy trees on the right hand bank, opposite to a bushy tree overgrowing a steel wicket gate on the left hand bank.

Proceeding upstream, just before reaching Abbey Bridge (grid ref 033431), clearance 14 ft/4.2 m, the River Isbourne will be seen flowing into the Avon on the right. Considerable shoaling occurs here particularly just downstream of the confluence, and the course followed should be to the left of the centre of the main river.

After the bridge we soon come to the Trust's overnight mooring at Waterside on the right bank, followed shortly by the Borough moorings at the Workman Gardens, opposite Lower Abbey Park, and in sight of Evesham's handsome Workman Bridge built over a century ago.

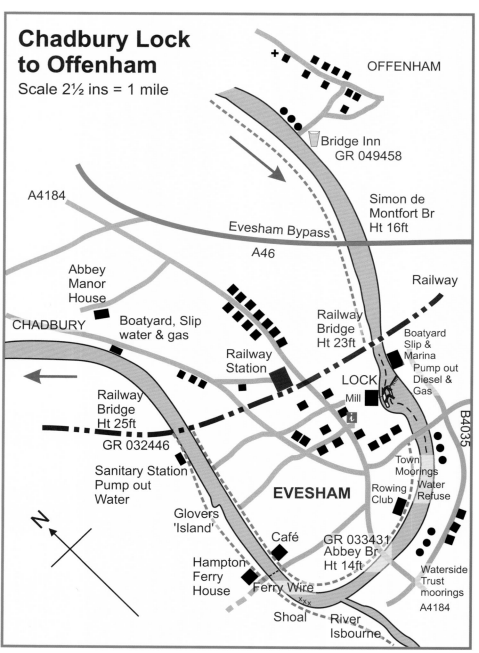

Chadbury Lock to Offenham

Scale 2½ ins = 1 mile

OFFENHAM

Bridge Inn
GR 049458

A4184

Simon de
Montfort Br
Ht 16ft

Evesham Bypass
A46

Abbey
Manor
House

Railway

CHADBURY

Boatyard, Slip
water & gas

Railway
Bridge
Ht 23ft

Boatyard
Slip &
Marina
Pump out
Diesel &
Gas

Railway
Station

LOCK

Mill

Railway
Bridge
Ht 25ft
GR 032446

B4035

Sanitary Station
Pump out
Water

Town
Moorings

EVESHAM

Rowing
Club

Water
Refuse

N

Glovers
'Island'

Café

GR 033431
Abbey Br
Ht 14ft

Hampton
Ferry
House

Waterside
Trust
moorings
A4184

Ferry Wire
xxx

Shoal
River
Isbourne

Chadbury to Offenham

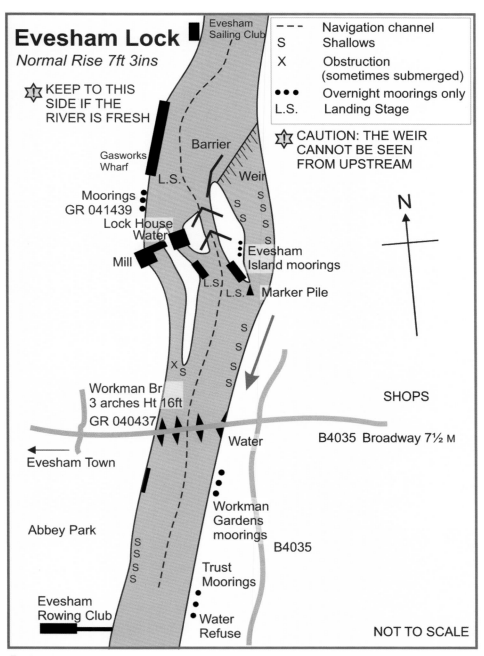

Evesham Lock

Normal Rise 7ft 3ins

☆ KEEP TO THIS SIDE IF THE RIVER IS FRESH

Legend:
- - -	Navigation channel
S	Shallows
X	Obstruction (sometimes submerged)
•••	Overnight moorings only
L.S.	Landing Stage

☆ CAUTION: THE WEIR CANNOT BE SEEN FROM UPSTREAM

Evesham Sailing Club

Gasworks Wharf

Barrier

Weir

L.S.

Moorings
GR 041439

Lock House

Water

Mill

Evesham Island moorings

L.S.

L.S. ▲ Marker Pile

N

S S S S S

Workman Br
3 arches Ht 16ft
GR 040437

SHOPS

Water

B4035 Broadway 7½ M

← Evesham Town

Workman Gardens moorings

B4035

Abbey Park

Trust Moorings

Evesham Rowing Club

Water
Refuse

NOT TO SCALE

Evesham Lock

Visitors Guide

The river through **EVESHAM** and in the straight stretch above Chadbury Lock is very suitable for rowing. The regular Spring Holiday Monday regatta attracts large entries from many parts of the country.

Evesham is a good shopping centre and there is some light industry, but the main source of its prosperity is the fruit growing and market gardening activity in the surrounding area. Much of this is carried out on a co-operative basis. All kinds of fruit and vegetable crops are grown, but the main ones are plums, sprouts and cabbage. Many crops are grown under glass and a visit to the surrounding area will show how the maximum output is obtained from any given space.

There are several places of interest within a few miles of Evesham. About 4 miles/6.4 km south is **BROADWAY** (grid ref 095375), a very picturesque village. This is on the fringe of the Cotswolds.

In a pocket of the hills, 3 miles/3.8 km south of Broadway is **SNOWSHILL** (grid ref 097337), a pretty village with a manor house containing a large collection of toys, musical instruments, etc. It is open to the public on most days of the summer months.
CHIPPING CAMPDEN is a typical Cotswold stone town, with a Jacobean market hall, 4 miles/6.4 km east of Broadway (grid ref 152392).

Nearby **DOVERS HILL** is National Trust property and a good lookout point over the Avon valley.

Evesham Sailing Club uses the part of the river upstream of the lock and sails all classes of dinghies.

Evesham Lock

Navigation Notes

Placed adjacent to the footpath opposite the Evesham Rowing Club, mains water and refuse bins are provided but the bank immediately downstream is obstructed.

Upstream of the Evesham Borough moorings and between Evesham Rowing Club and the Workman Bridge (grid ref 040437), clearance 16 ft/4.8 m, there is a dredged navigation channel 5 ft/1.5 m deep by approximately 30 ft/9 m wide up the centre of the river. Elsewhere the depth may be less, therefore caution should be exercised.

The centre arch only of the Workman Bridge should be used. Upstream from the Workman Bridge the channel lies slightly to the west (island side) of centre. Shallows exist where marked on the plan.

On no account should craft venture into the weir pool. If EVESHAM LOCK, which is of minimum length, is "against" craft proceeding upstream they should wait at the landing stage below the lock. Waiting and mooring on the west (island side) bank is strictly prohibited without permission.

There is a resident lock keeper at this lock (telephone 01386 446511) who should be consulted if visitor's moorings are required. Mains water is available at the lock.

Upstream the channel lies in the centre of the river with shallows along the weir crest. There are moorings along the towpath at the Gasworks Wharf by arrangement with the lock keeper. When the river is running "fresh" (ie higher than normal level due to heavy rain) it is advisable to keep to the bank side when passing the weir and boats proceeding downstream should hold back and give way to boats leaving the lock until these are clear of the weir crest.

When travelling downstream the crest of Evesham Weir is invisible. Craft should proceed with care keeping well to the right hand bank.

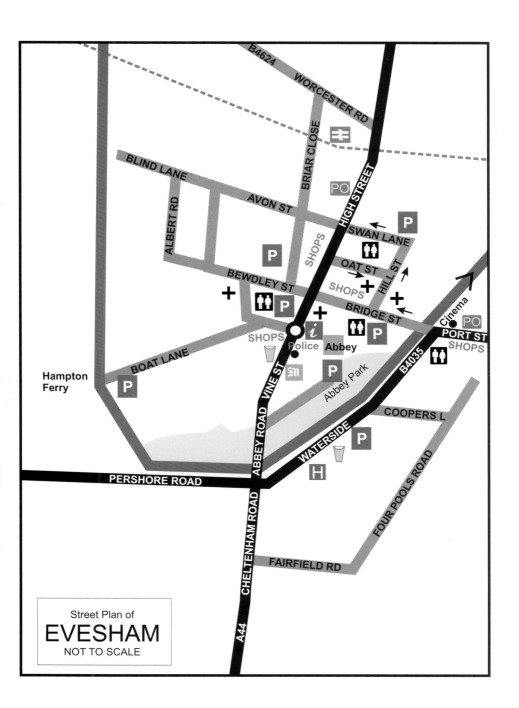

Street Plan of
EVESHAM
NOT TO SCALE

Workman Bridge, Evesham

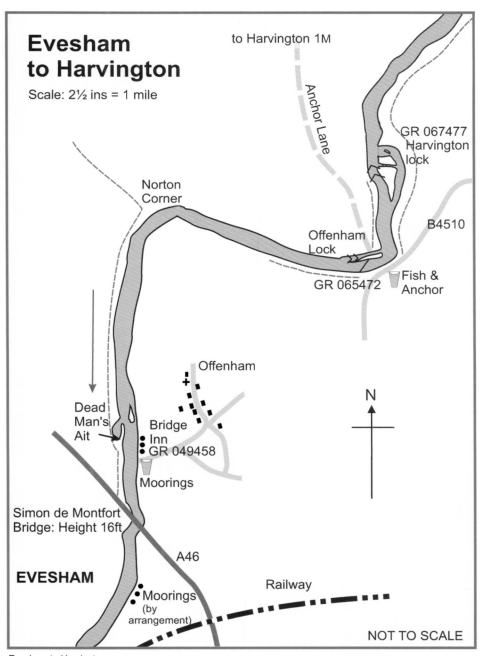

Evesham to Harvington

Scale: 2½ ins = 1 mile

to Harvington 1M

Anchor Lane

GR 067477
Harvington lock

Norton Corner

Offenham Lock

B4510

GR 065472

Fish & Anchor

Offenham

N

Dead Man's Ait

Bridge Inn
GR 049458

Moorings

Simon de Montfort Bridge: Height 16ft

A46

EVESHAM

Railway

Moorings
(by arrangement)

NOT TO SCALE

Evesham to Harvington

Visitors Guide

Evesham to Harvington

After leaving Evesham, the Navigation passes beneath the London, Oxford and Hereford railway to Offenham, once the headquarters of Offa, of Dyke fame, the Bridge Inn and the aptly named "Dead Man's Ait". On 4 August 1265, the army of Simon de Montfort, "Father of the House of Commons", trapped within the loop of the Avon, was destroyed by the forces of Henry III under his son, a brilliant tactician, who later as Edward 1, subjected the Welsh and Scots to English rule.

In "The murther of Evesham - for battle non it was", Simon, his son and 5,000 of his followers were killed. Some attempted to escape across the river at Offenham, few succeeded and in the 18th century, at Dead Man's Ait, a large quantity of human bones was unearthed.

At the second battle of Evesham, in May 1645, a Royalist garrison surrendered to a besieging force of Roundheads.

These and other events in the history of Evesham are well documented in the museum which occupies the almonry of the former abbey.

The bridge has long ago disappeared, perhaps cleared away by the original navigators, and replaced by a ferry which, sadly, no longer operates.

Offenham Lock

Navigation Notes

Evesham to Harvington

(See map on page 57)

On leaving Evesham Lock, the river heads right, across the top of the weir - so craft need to keep left, well away from it.
When travelling downstream, boaters cannot see the weir until they are nearly upon it, so craft should keep to the right and look out for the long weir crest on their left.

Shortly after the lock, proceeding upstream, Evesham Sailing Club is to the left (opposite a caravan park on the right-hand bank) and craft should keep a look-out for the club's sailing boats on the river.

We then pass Evesham Marina on the right (offering water, pump-out, gas and overnight moorings), followed immediately after by a railway bridge where vessels should take the main (left-hand) arch.
Above the Simon de Montfort Bridge (carrying the A46 Evesham bypass), Badsey Brook joins the river on the right.

We are now in the heart of the Vale of Evesham's market gardening countryside.

At Offenham, moorings are available by arrangement at the Bridge Inn, which is on the right-hand bank. Having passed the village of Offenham, craft have to negotiate a sharp right-hand bend, Norton Corner, where you should keep to the outside where the navigation is deeper.
Proceeding upstream, OFFENHAM LOCK channel (grid ref. 065472) is on the left, with moorings each side on the approach.

On leaving the lock, there are good overnight moorings on both banks, plus a water point, refuse disposal facilities and a sanitary station. Craft then pass under William Smith Bridge, which is followed by further moorings on each bank.

Offenham & Harvington Locks

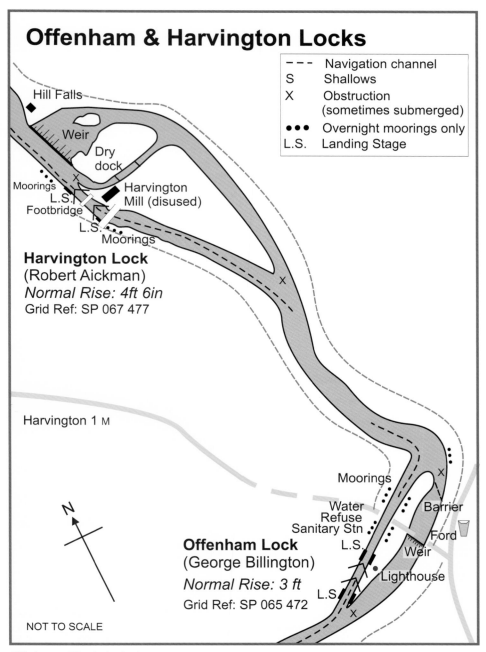

– – –	Navigation channel
S	Shallows
X	Obstruction (sometimes submerged)
•••	Overnight moorings only
L.S.	Landing Stage

Hill Falls

Weir

Dry dock

Moorings

L.S.

Footbridge

Harvington Mill (disused)

L.S.

Moorings

Harvington Lock
(Robert Aickman)
Normal Rise: 4ft 6in
Grid Ref: SP 067 477

Harvington 1 M

N

Moorings

Water
Refuse
Sanitary Stn

L.S.

Offenham Lock
(George Billington)
Normal Rise: 3 ft
Grid Ref: SP 065 472

L.S.

Barrier

Ford

Weir

Lighthouse

NOT TO SCALE

Offenham and Harvington Locks

Visitors Guide

When GEORGE BILLINGTON donated the cost of building a lock on the site at Offenham he did not have long to live. Volunteers from Gloucester Gaol, the Waterways Recovery Group and others set to work and within six weeks the lock was completed. George, who had followed progress with eager interest, died a week later.

Alongside the Fish and Anchor Inn is a causeway which, in 1901, was raised to serve the railway station at Harvington, an illegal obstruction of navigation which, in the interests of local relations, the Trust retained as a weir and bypassed with the lock and lock cuts. The old railway station became for some years the Upper Avon Navigation Trust's headquarters.

HARVINGTON LOCK is a national memorial to Robert Aickman who for many years led the battle to save the inland waterways from hostile official attitudes and public indifference.

The original Robert Aickman lock, the first of the restoration, was built by volunteers including men from Gloucester Gaol and Royal Engineers from Belfast, upon the remains of the 17th century structure - a mistake never to be repeated! The old foundations were impenetrable.

Harvington (originally known as Herverton) was first mentioned in the Anglo Saxon charters of 709 AD. St James church is believed to be over 500 years old and has the only copper spire in the Vale.

Navigation Notes

On the right above the lock weir is The Fish & Anchor pub, which has customer moorings - but care must be taken when passing the crest of the weir to moor up here.
The lock cut then bears left to re-join the main river.

At HARVINGTON LOCK (grid ref. 067477), moorings are on the left below the lock, with further moorings above. It is overlooked by the old Harvington Mill. Behind the mill is the old lock basin, which has been converted into a dry dock - the entrance channel is on the right above the current lock.

Coming out of Harvington Lock, steer diagonally across the basin, keeping to your left across the top of the weir.

Offenham Lock

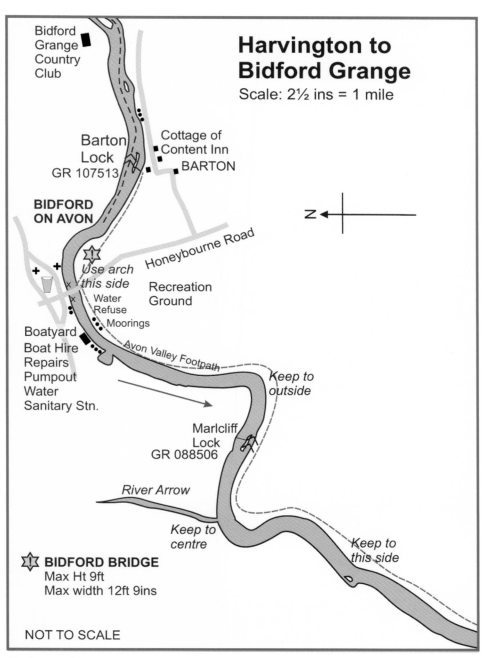

Bidford
Grange
Country
Club

Barton
Lock
GR 107513

Cottage of
Content Inn
BARTON

BIDFORD
ON AVON

Honeybourne Road

Use arch
this side

Recreation
Ground

Water
Refuse
Moorings

Boatyard
Boat Hire
Repairs
Pumpout
Water
Sanitary Stn.

Avon Valley Footpath

Keep to
outside

Marlcliff
Lock
GR 088506

River Arrow

Keep to
centre

Keep to
this side

BIDFORD BRIDGE
Max Ht 9ft
Max width 12ft 9ins

NOT TO SCALE

Harvington to Bidford Grange

Scale: 2½ ins = 1 mile

N

Harvington to Bidford Grange

Visitors Guide

Harvington to Bidford Grange

The Trust was required by the water authority to remove Cleeve weir. This led to heavy and expensive dredging and bank protection work up to the site of **MARLCLIFF LOCK**.

The subsoil, marl, resembles diamond-hard rubber which shrugs off huge machines and heavy explosive charges. Royal Engineers from Belfast eventually blasted and gouged out the chamber which was then lined with piles.

The original gates (replaced in the 1980s) were salvaged from the demolished Runcorn flight of locks.

The Trust was permitted to build only a low weir to replace Cleeve weir, and the consequent low water levels led to serious difficulties above the lock and at Bidford Bridge.

The work was paid for by the Inland Waterways Association and the land given by the Birmingham Anglers Association.

The site of **BIDFORD ON AVON** MOORINGS was given by the Duchess Dudley Trust which, in the 18th century, sent out curates to rescue English maidens from the harems of the East. Apparently a singularly unsuccessful enterprise!

A riverside footpath to Offenham and Barton runs alongside this mooring.

The demolition of Cleeve weir led to heavy dredging and the lowering of the foundations of the navigation arch of Bidford Bridge, built by the monks of Alcester in 1482.

Navigation Notes

Harvington to Bidford Grange
(See map on page 61)

Passing the site of the old Cleeve Lock, the remains of the chamber can be seen on the left-hand bank and those of the weir on the right. The river then bends right, with the River Arrow joining the Avon to the left. The navigation becomes shallow at the confluence of the two rivers, due to silt being carried down the Arrow, so craft need to maintain a centre course.

Approaching MARLCLIFF LOCK (grid ref. 088506) the weir is to the left, so craft must carefully navigate to the lock channel on the right-hand side. The navigable channel narrows and can be shallow.

On approach, the main lock mooring is to the left and there is also a small mooring on the right. Leaving the lock there is a very narrow cut - care must be taken and a low speed maintained, especially if boats are approaching from upstream.

Keep right as you pass the crest of the weir on the left, giving way to boats coming downstream.

Approaching the lock when travelling downstream, slow right down and take extreme care - but be sure to keep up sufficient revs to maintain steerage and keep clear of the weir on your right. Bear to your left into the lock channel.

Bidford on Avon

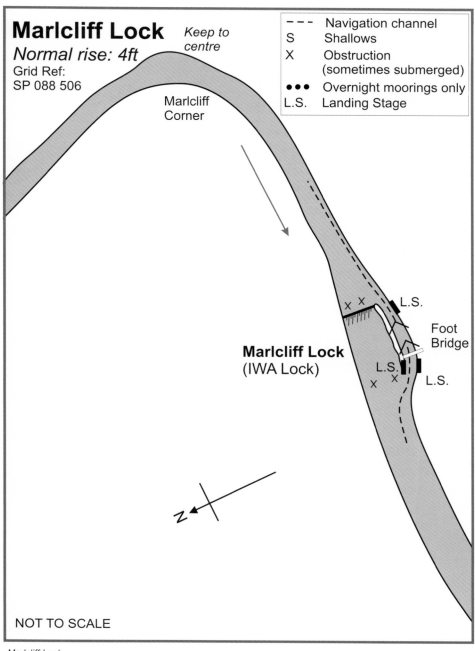

Marlcliff Lock

Keep to centre

Normal rise: 4ft

Grid Ref:
SP 088 506

Marlcliff
Corner

	Navigation channel
S	Shallows
X	Obstruction (sometimes submerged)
●●●	Overnight moorings only
L.S.	Landing Stage

X X   L.S.

Marlcliff Lock
(IWA Lock)

Foot
Bridge

L.S.

X   X   L.S.

N

NOT TO SCALE

Marlcliff Lock

Visitors Guide

Beyond Bidford bridge, the Roman ford, which carried Buckle Street (part of Ryknild Street - the old Roman road) on its way to Alcester, had to be breached to permit navigation.

The church of St Lawrence dates from 1276 but was replaced in 1835.

In the square is the former Falcon Inn, where according to tradition, in 1616 William Shakespeare indulged in a drinking bout against Bidford which Stratford lost.

Whilst wandering home and sleeping under "Shakespeare's crab" on Tower Hill, the bard caught the chill which led to his death.

Upon the neighbouring Cleeve Hill, in 1811, the largest hoard of Roman coin found in Great Britain was unearthed.

BIDFORD ON AVON is a large picturesque village with four inns, including the Bidford Riverside Eaterie which is a newly opened riverside brasserie on the banks of the River Avon, next to the bridge.

BARTON LOCK was donated by Elsie and Hiram Billington, the parents of George Billington and was built in six weeks by boys from Hewell Grange Borstal, Redditch, and is unusual in having three walls in order to enclose the lock island.

The original wooden gates were salvaged from the Thames.

BARTON is an unspoilt hamlet with an interesting pub inaccessible by boat but a pleasant field path runs from Bidford.

A short distance upstream the Navigation passes through the remains of Grange weir and thus alongside the sites of the former lock and grist and paper mills.

Bidford Grange was once the scene of much rural industry but is now a golf club.

Navigation Notes

For 1,000 yards upstream of Marlcliff Lock, craft should keep to the right of centre and proceed carefully during normal summer levels, as the river can be very shallow.

After the lock, there is a sharp bend to the left, Marlcliff Corner, where a centre course should be maintained. There then follows a nice straight, deep run.

As craft approach Bidford, there is a marina - The Moorings - on the left, followed by Bidford Boats, a hire fleet and boatyard, also on the left. It offers pump-out facilities, a sanitary station, water and overnight moorings on request.

Shortly after, on the left, there are moorings at The Frog and Bulrush pub, just before Bidford Bridge. Next to the pub is The Bridge restaurant, which also offers customer moorings - but these should be approached with caution as the navigation is very shallow here.

On the right before the bridge is the recreation ground, where there are overnight moorings, public toilets, water and refuse disposal facilities.

At Bidford Bridge, hold over to the small right-hand arch when heading upstream. Care must be taken due to the strong current and craft must give way to vessels coming downstream.

There follows a sharp right-hand bend and the river then bears left before coming to BARTON LOCK (grid ref. 107513), where the lock channel is on the left. Above the lock, the lock mooring, a winding hole and overnight moorings are to the left. Craft should keep left on leaving the lock

After re-joining the main river channel from the lock, there is a large caravan park on the right. Heading upstream, Barton Cruisers (which offers moorings) is on the right, before we reach a small island where craft should hold to the left. Then, about 600 metres upstream, the river splits and craft need to take the right-hand channel.

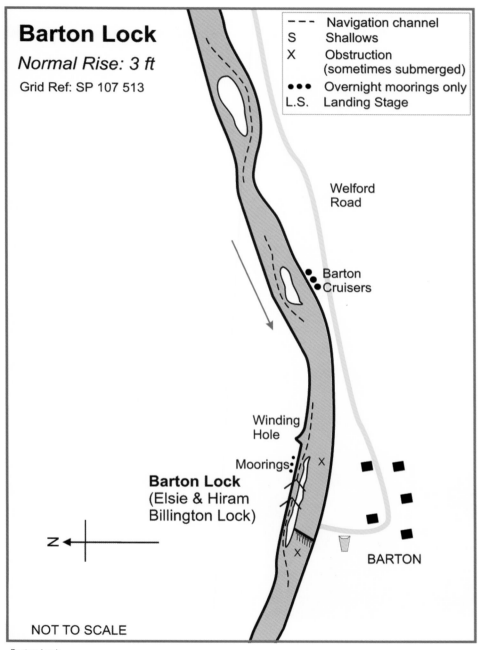

Barton Lock

Normal Rise: 3 ft

Grid Ref: SP 107 513

– – –	Navigation channel
S	Shallows
X	Obstruction (sometimes submerged)
●●●	Overnight moorings only
L.S.	Landing Stage

Welford Road

Barton Cruisers

Winding Hole

Moorings

Barton Lock (Elsie & Hiram Billington Lock)

N

BARTON

NOT TO SCALE

Barton Lock

Visitors Guide

Bidford Grange to Weston

The cost of the Bidford Grange Lock was donated by the Pilgrim Trust and was hand built with thousands of steel-reinforced concrete blocks by men from Gloucester Gaol.

Although the site was soft, floods frequent and avalanches commonplace, the resulting structure was effective and pleasing to the eye.

Upstream the river is particularly attractive as it passes Hillborough Manor, Shakespeare's "haunted Hillboro", to where, it is said, Charles II escaped after the battle of Worcester in 1651 and where his treasure was buried. It is yet to be found.

A footpath links the lock to Barton and Bidford.

Bidford on Avon

Navigation Notes

Bidford Grange to Weston
(See map facing)

Heading upstream, the river bears to the right, passing the entrance to the old lock channel before arriving at BIDFORD GRANGE LOCK (grid ref. 122517). Bear to the right to enter the lock channel, where the lock mooring is on the right.

At WELFORD LOCK (grid ref. 144521), bear left into the lock channel and beware of the current from the weir to the right, which can be very fierce.
It is quite a deep lock so, coming upstream, make sure you hold the boat firmly because the turbulence in the lock is considerable.

On leaving the lock, the lock mooring is on the left and overnight moorings on the right (but they offer no access to Welford village). Bear left as you re-join the main river channel.

Above Welford are private moorings, then a sharp right-hand bend, followed on the right by the entrance to a marina, Welford Boat Station (which offers riverbank overnight moorings on request, with access to Welford, as well as boat repairs and a chandlery). Do not enter the marina basins, as they are reserved for long-term moorings.

The river then forks and craft should take the right-hand channel past the island immediately before Binton Bridges, then take the left arch as indicated by the blue and white arrow signs.

Coming downstream on the approach to Binton Bridges, slow down considerably and bear left, taking care not to follow the other (un-navigable) channels - and take the right-hand arch as indicated.

On the right just after the bridge is The Four Alls pub, where there is limited overnight mooring available by arrangement. There follows a caravan park on the right-hand bank, after which the river bears sharply to the left, then to the right.

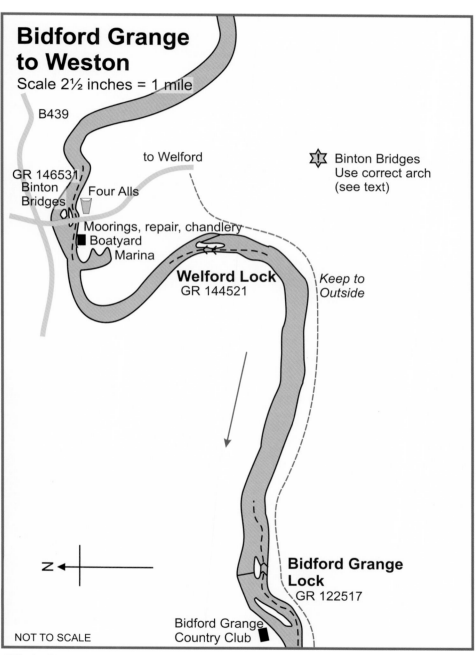

Bidford Grange to Weston

Scale 2½ inches = 1 mile

B439

to Welford

Binton Bridges
Use correct arch
(see text)

GR 146531
Binton
Bridges

Four Alls

Moorings, repair, chandlery

Boatyard
Marina

Welford Lock
GR 144521

*Keep to
Outside*

N

**Bidford Grange
Lock**
GR 122517

Bidford Grange
Country Club

NOT TO SCALE

Bidford to Weston

Navigating through Bidford and Binton Bridges at time of "fresh" water

Only the largest arch in these ancient multi-arched bridges should be used for navigation.

Whilst not wishing to over-emphasise the danger which develops at these bridges at such times when the river has risen above normal level it is nevertheless necessary to indicate the danger that does exist.

Naturally, as a result of heavy rainfall over a long period the river will rise and the rate of flow increases. This in turn lessens headroom beneath the bridge, and develops turbulence in the area immediately downstream and upstream of the bridge piers.

IT IS ADVISABLE ON SUCH OCCASIONS TO WAIT A DAY OR TWO TO ALLOW THE RIVER TO FALL AND FOR BETTER NAVIGATION CONDITIONS. If navigation is attempted, then be sure to "square-up" to the centre arch so that the craft cannot be swept against the piers, or if travelling downstream, to be swept broadside across the bridge.

At all times, craft navigating upstream should give way to those travelling downstream.

IF IN DOUBT, STOP, MOOR UP AND SEEK ADVICE.

Visitors Guide

The Navigation passes through the ruins of Lower Welford Lock and its weir, the destruction of which led to great difficulties with the stone which formed the river bed upstream. The piles of the lock chamber had to be driven through two layers of the same material.

The new **WELFORD** LOCK was paid for by the Cadbury family.

The remains of Upper Welford Lock are buried in the island and until recently a corn mill stood alongside the weir.

Welford, which may be reached from Binton Bridges, has the interesting early church of St Peter, a village stores, many Tudor half-timbered and thatched cottages, three pubs, footpaths and a soaring maypole, the tallest in Britain at 65ft/20metres. A walk up Cress Hill provides panoramic views of the river and surrounding countryside.

In Weston upon Avon the ancient church of All Saints has windows with paintings of little roofed salt-carrying boats.

Close by the Navigation passes through the ruins of Lower Luddington Lock and weir, whose removal led to extensive hard dredging when restoring the navigation, as re-instatement of the lock was not permitted.

Boat approaching Barton Lock

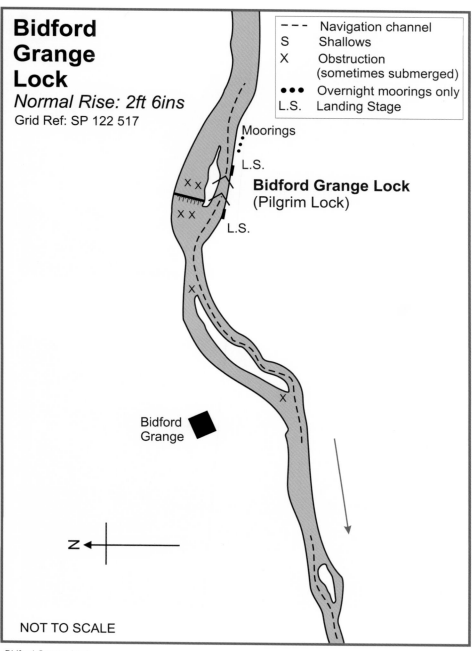

Bidford
Grange
Lock

Normal Rise: 2ft 6ins
Grid Ref: SP 122 517

– – –	Navigation channel
S	Shallows
X	Obstruction (sometimes submerged)
•••	Overnight moorings only
L.S.	Landing Stage

Moorings

L.S.

Bidford Grange Lock
(Pilgrim Lock)

X X

X X

L.S.

X

X

Bidford
Grange

Z ←

NOT TO SCALE

Bidford Grange Lock

Canoeing below Stratford Trinity Lock

The Royal Shakespeare Theatre, Stratford upon Avon

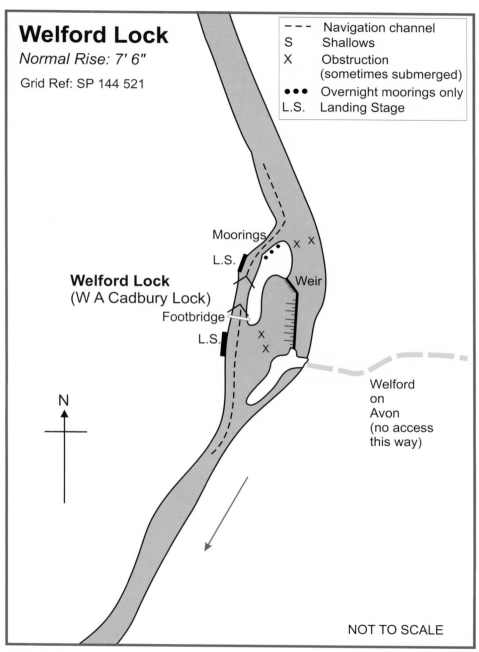

Welford Lock

Normal Rise: 7' 6"

Grid Ref: SP 144 521

	Navigation channel
– – –	Navigation channel
S	Shallows
X	Obstruction (sometimes submerged)
●●●	Overnight moorings only
L.S.	Landing Stage

Moorings

L.S.

Welford Lock
(W A Cadbury Lock)

Footbridge

L.S.

Weir

X X

X
X

Welford
on
Avon
(no access
this way)

N

NOT TO SCALE

Welford Lock

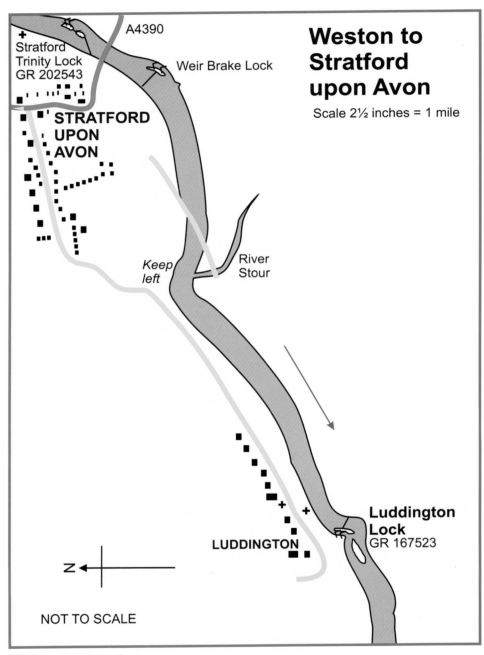

Weston to Stratford upon Avon

Scale 2½ inches = 1 mile

A4390

+ Stratford Trinity Lock
GR 202543

Weir Brake Lock

STRATFORD UPON AVON

Keep left

River Stour

LUDDINGTON

Luddington Lock
GR 167523

Z

NOT TO SCALE

Weston to Stratford upon Avon

Visitors Guide

Weston to Stratford upon Avon

LUDDINGTON LOCK was donated by the family of Stan Clover who worked untiringly for the Navigation along with other volunteers without whose assistance the Trust could not have achieved its aim.

With its weir it was built by the men from Gloucester Gaol. Seven-ton piling hammers were needed to break through layers of stone.

The entrance to the former round Upper Luddington Lock lies alongside the new structure.

The former cut is now a basin and a pleasant overnight mooring from which a footpath runs along the riverside to Stratford upon Avon.

Luddington church was built in 1871 to replace a structure which was burned down much earlier and in which, reputedly, Shakespeare married Anne Hathaway.

A short distance upstream, near the confluence with the River Stour, is a rock slab through which the navigation channel had to be cut.

Further on extensive silt bank and the remains of a former railway structure had to be cleared with explosives. The steel former railway bridge now carries a footpath and cycle track.

WEIR BRAKE (GORDON GRAY) LOCK commemorates the contribution of a then anonymous donor whose generosity launched the restoration scheme.

The biggest, the best and the last of the new locks was built in thirty-eight days by boys from Hewell Grange Borstal and other volunteers, who then quickly built the weir.

The sites were given by Edgar and Mabel Jones whose generosity is commemorated by the bridge across the chamber.

A footpath runs to Stratford upon Avon and to Clifford Chambers.

Navigation Notes

Weston to Stratford upon Avon
(See map facing)

The river becomes quite shallow and narrow, as we approach Luddington.

Bear left into the LUDDINGTON LOCK channel (grid ref. 167523). Above the lock, as we re-join the main river channel, overnight moorings are on the left. There is also a water point, refuse disposal and a sanitary station.

Just over a mile after Luddington Lock, craft should keep to the left as they pass the confluence with the River Stour on the right. There then follows the old railway bridge, which is now a foot and cycle path.

Bear right into WEIR BRAKE LOCK channel (grid ref. 198536), where there is a small lock mooring on the left. Above the lock, there are overnight moorings to the right. Coming downstream, take care to bear to your left into the lock channel.

Proceeding upstream, shortly after the lock, take the right-hand channel when the river forks at "Sausage Island" (so called because of its shape). After the A4390 road bridge, craft pass under the footbridge to Trinity Church before arriving at STRATFORD TRINITY LOCK (grid ref. 202543). On the approach to the lock, the two weirs are at right angles to the river. Take care when passing them: when the river is in flood, they can be very dangerous.

Soon after the weirs, bear left into the lock. The lock mooring is on the left below the lock. When coming downstream, the lock channel is to your left.

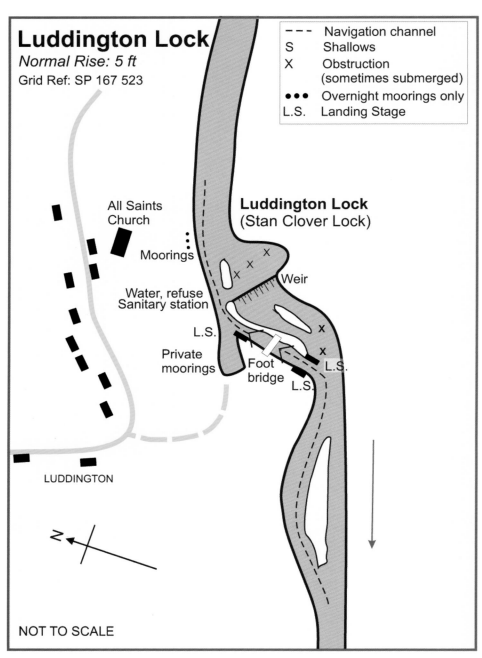

Luddington Lock

Visitors Guide

On 1 June 1974, the helicopter carrying HM Queen Elizabeth, the Queen Mother, landed at the lock from where her majesty travelled in the narrowboat "Jubilee" into Stratford, ceremonially to re-open the Upper Avon Navigation.

A short distance upstream the Navigation passes through a blue brick former railway bridge upon which the royal train rested when, on 11 July 1964, the Queen Mother opened the restored Stratford Canal.

STRATFORD TRINITY LOCK,
commemorating the generosity of Colin P Witter, was the most difficult to build because of its unusual depth and the unstable nature of the ground - a silt pit. The work was undertaken by men from Gloucester Gaol and other volunteers. The remains of the former lock lie beneath the mound upon which stands the monument commemorating the success of the restoration scheme. It was unveiled by Queen Elizabeth, the Queen Mother, on 1 June 1974.

Upstream is Holy Trinity Church which accommodates Shakespeare's tomb, and the Royal Shakespeare Theatre which played a prominent part in the events of 1 June 1974, and the entrance to the Stratford upon Avon Canal. The Royal Shakespeare Company operates a number of theatres in Stratford upon Avon.

Access to the town from the riverside footpath is provided by a footbridge (first built in 1599), the tramway bridge (abandoned in 1926) and a manually-propelled chain ferry.

Stratford upon Avon also lists Shakespeare's House, Shakespeare's birthplace, Ann Hathaway's Cottage, Mary Arden's House, Hall's Croft, Nash's House, Bancroft Basin and gardens and the Butterfly Farm amongst its many tourist attractions.

Stratford upon Avon riverside

Trip boat in Stratford upon Avon

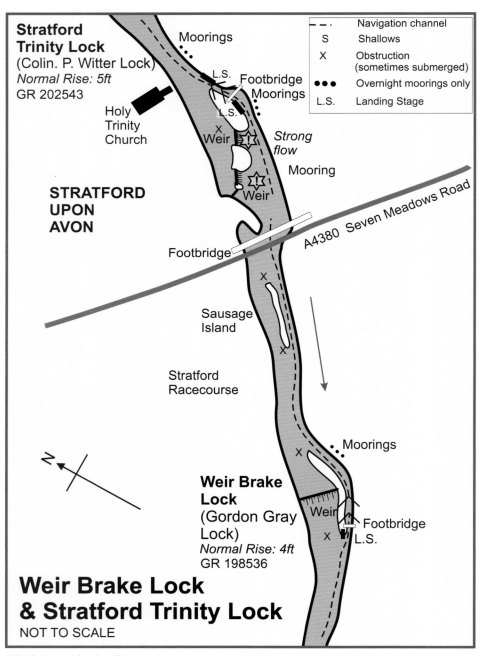

Stratford Trinity Lock
(Colin. P. Witter Lock)
Normal Rise: 5ft
GR 202543

Holy Trinity Church

STRATFORD UPON AVON

Moorings

L.S. Footbridge
Moorings

L.S.

X Weir

Strong flow

Weir

Mooring

A4380 Seven Meadows Road

Footbridge

X

Sausage Island

X

Stratford Racecourse

X

Moorings

X

Weir Brake Lock
(Gordon Gray Lock)
Normal Rise: 4ft
GR 198536

Weir
Footbridge
X L.S.

N

	Navigation channel
S	Shallows
X	Obstruction (sometimes submerged)
●●●	Overnight moorings only
L.S.	Landing Stage

Weir Brake Lock & Stratford Trinity Lock
NOT TO SCALE

Wier Brake and Stratford Trinity Locks

Stratford Trinity Lock

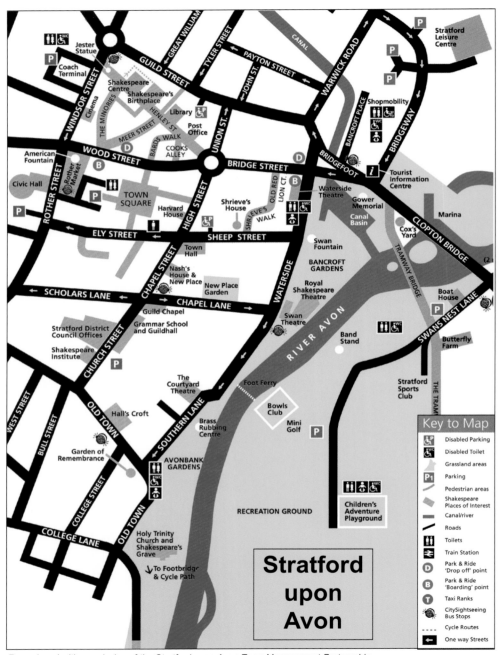

Stratford upon Avon

Key to Map
- Disabled Parking
- Disabled Toilet
- Grassland areas
- Parking
- Pedestrian areas
- Shakespeare Places of Interest
- Canal/river
- Roads
- Toilets
- Train Station
- Park & Ride 'Drop off' point
- Park & Ride 'Boarding' point
- Taxi Ranks
- CitySightseeing Bus Stops
- Cycle Routes
- One way Streets

Reproduced with permission of the Stratford upon Avon Town Management Partnership

78

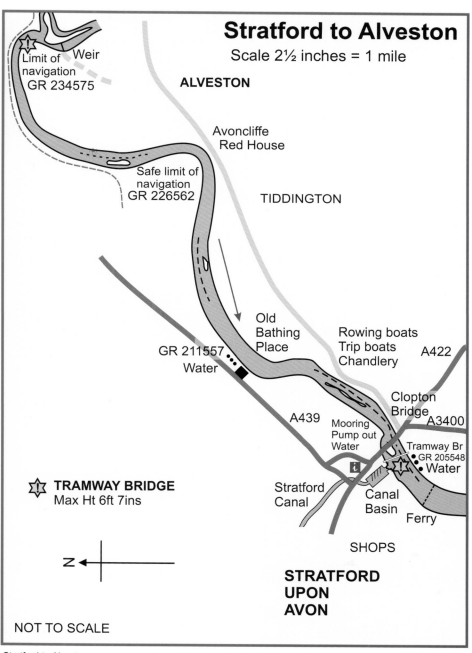

Stratford to Alveston
Scale 2½ inches = 1 mile

Limit of navigation
GR 234575

Weir

ALVESTON

Avoncliffe
Red House

Safe limit of
navigation
GR 226562

TIDDINGTON

Old
Bathing
Place

GR 211557
Water

Rowing boats
Trip boats
Chandlery

A422

A439

Clopton
Bridge

A3400

Mooring
Pump out
Water

Tramway Br
GR 205548
Water

Stratford
Canal

Canal
Basin

Ferry

☆ **TRAMWAY BRIDGE**
Max Ht 6ft 7ins

Z ←

SHOPS

**STRATFORD
UPON
AVON**

NOT TO SCALE

Stratford to Alveston

Visitors Guide

Stratford upon Avon to Alveston

The bay at the OLD BATHING PLACE had long been an aquatic playground for locals and visitors alike, when, in the mid-1930s, diving boards, a chute, changing huts and a floating safety boom were installed and bathing suits were offered for hire (wholesale gentlemen's £1.6s.0d per dozen, ladies' £1.12.6d!)

Those facilities survived a world war but, in the 1950s, whispers of polio brought about their demise.

The site continues to provide facilities for boaters, anglers and walkers.

The Navigation continues upstream to Alveston weir and sluice, the present head of the navigation where once stood a magnificent water mill.

About twelve miles upstream of Alveston the Grand Union Canal spans the Avon at Warwick. Access to and the linking of these two waterways is the ultimate aim of the Stratford and Warwick Waterways Trust.

*The New Place, Stratford upon Avon
(Shakespeare's final home)*

Navigation Notes

Stratford upon Avon to Alveston
(See map on page 79)

After Stratford Trinity Lock, there follows a long stretch of moorings on the right and craft should keep a look-out for rowing and trip boats at this popular spot. Also look out for the chain ferry across the river, which is busy in peak season.

Moorings continue on the right-hand bank, with a water point halfway along. Proceeding upstream, we now enter the centre of Stratford, with the theatres to our left and the recreation ground to the right.

Boaters wishing to ascend the lock into the Stratford Canal should note that they may need to drop a crew member off on the right bank before turning toward the lock. They then have to make their way on foot via Tramway bridge and Bancroft gardens to the lock.

Immediately after passing the lock to the left which takes craft up into Bancroft Basin and on to the Southern Section of the Stratford Canal, we pass under Tramway Bridge, where the navigable arch is indicated by signs and clearance is only 6ft 7in.

There are private moorings on the right, with rowing boats for hire and trip boats (at Avon Boating, which also has a chandlery). Bear right past the island in the middle of the river, then through the navigable arch (as indicated by signs) of Clopton Bridge.

The entrance to a boatyard, Stratford Marina (offering mooring, pump-out and water), is to the left, then craft must keep right past a series of small islands. There is a sharp S-bend, followed by the Old Bathing Place on the left, which offers public moorings and a water point.

Care should be taken as the river starts to become more narrow and shallow. Soon we pass under the access bridge for a caravan park, followed by a sharp left bend at Tiddington, where boats drawing more than 18 inches and longer than 30 feet are advised not to proceed any further.

Small craft with a shallow draft may continue on to Hatton Rock, where there is a sign indicating the end of the navigation.

Tramway Bridge, Stratford upon Avon

The Old Bathing Place, Stratford upon Avon

RIVER MILEAGE CHART   (1 mile = 1.6 km)

	River Severn	Avon Lock, Tewkesbury	Strensham Lock	Nafford Lock	Pershore Lock	Wyre Lock	Fladbury Lock	Chadbury Lock	Evesham Lock	Offenham Lock	Harvington Lock	Marlcliff Lock	Barton Lock	Bidford Grange Lock	Welford Lock	Luddington Lock	Weir Brake Lock	Stratford Trinity Lock
Alveston Weir	47.2	47.0	41.4	38.7	32.6	31.6	27.2	24.5	21.5	17.8	17.1	14.3	12.4	9.8	8.6	6.8	4.0	3.9
Stratford Trinity Lock	43.3	43.1	37.5	34.8	28.7	27.7	23.3	20.6	17.6	13.9	13.2	10.4	8.5	5.9	4.7	2.9	0.1	-
Weir Brake Lock	43.2	43.0	37.4	34.7	28.6	27.6	23.2	20.5	17.5	13.8	13.1	10.3	8.4	5.8	4.6	2.8	-	
Luddington Lock	40.4	40.2	34.6	31.9	25.8	24.8	20.4	17.7	14.7	11.0	10.3	7.5	5.6	3.0	1.8	-		
Welford Lock	38.6	38.4	32.8	29.1	24.0	23.0	18.6	15.9	12.9	9.2	8.5	5.7	3.8	1.2	-			
Bidford Grange Lock	37.4	37.2	31.6	27.9	22.8	21.8	17.4	14.7	11.7	8.0	7.3	4.5	2.6	-				
Barton Lock	34.8	34.6	29.0	25.3	20.2	19.2	14.8	12.1	9.1	5.4	4.7	1.9	-					
Marlcliff Lock	32.9	32.7	27.1	23.4	18.3	17.3	12.9	10.2	7.2	3.5	2.8	-						
Harvington Lock	30.1	29.9	24.3	20.6	15.5	14.5	10.1	7.4	4.4	0.7	-							
Offenham Lock	29.4	29.2	23.6	19.9	14.8	13.8	9.4	6.7	3.7	-								
Evesham Lock	25.7	25.5	19.9	16.2	11.1	10.1	5.7	3.0	-									
Chadbury Lock	22.7	22.5	16.9	13.2	8.1	7.1	2.7	-										
Fladbury Lock	20.0	19.8	14.2	10.5	5.4	4.4	-											
Wyre Lock	15.6	15.4	9.8	6.1	1.0	-												
Pershore Lock	14.6	14.4	8.8	5.1	-													
Nafford Lock	9.5	9.3	3.7	-														
Strensham Lock	5.8	5.6	-															
Avon Lock Tewkesbury	0.2																	

82

HISTORY of the Avon Navigation

In 1636 the history of navigation on the Avon commenced when letters patent were granted by Charles the First to William Sandys of Fladbury who used his private fortune, estimated between £20,000 and £40,000, in purchasing the necessary land and property and in the construction of sluices, weirs, channels and locks to make the Avon navigable from Tewkesbury to Stratford.

In 1758 the Lower Avon (ie the 26 miles/42 km from Tewkesbury to Evesham) was acquired by George Perrott who discovered that the locks were in such poor condition that in places passage was impossible, and it became necessary to close the Navigation for some months while repairs were carried out. Over a period of ten years some £4,000 had to be spent in restoration.

In 1830 the Lower Avon was leased to the Worcester and Birmingham (Canal) Company for £1,000 per annum for 21 years, during which period they spent considerable sums on repairs. On expiry the lease was renewed but a lower rental was negotiated as the profits of operation had fallen steadily throughout the first term, and when the railway linking Evesham to Gloucester was opened the Lower Avon commenced making substantial losses each year and consequently the lease was terminated finally in 1872.

The declining standard led to the formation in 1899 of the River Avon Improvement Association, which successfully persuaded the Local Authorities in 1903 to call a public enquiry into the state of the navigation, but unfortunately the Commissioners' recommendations, which would have led to restoration, were not accepted.

By 1914 the income from the Navigation was insufficient to carry out proper maintenance and the traffic operators, together with mill owners and Local Councils, were obliged to undertake essential repairs at their own expense.

In 1919 local borough and county councils became concerned about the condition of the Avon, and set up a joint committee to draw up a scheme for restoring the whole river for submission to the Ministry of Transport. The cost was claimed to be prohibitive, and the scheme was dropped.

In 1924, The Lower Avon Navigation Company Ltd was formed and acquired the Navigation by purchasing the Perrott interest. Over £2,000 had to be spent on immediate repairs and by 1931 it was decided that the Navigation would have to be abandoned as the revenue had become too small to maintain the river in a navigable condition. In order to obtain powers to increase revenue by various charges to river users, a last effort was made by introducing a Private Bill into Parliament. Possibly because these powers were being sought by a private company, they were opposed by Local Authorities and others, and the Bill was rejected.

During World War II the river became unnavigable above Pershore, and continued to deteriorate, so that by 1949, as Strensham Lock was rapidly becoming impassable, the river was virtually closed for navigation. Only a grain barge "Pisgah" managed to trade to Pershore Mill continuously into the post restoration period until she ceased running in 1972.

Since the days of Charles the First, there have been three names prominently associated with navigation on the Avon - William Sandys, who started it, the Perrotts who developed it, and C D Barwell who saved it.

Pershore New Bridge

In 1949, C D Barwell entered the scene when the Navigation of the Lower Avon was fast approaching complete, final and irrevocable disintegration. In this year, the Inland Waterways Association called a conference of people concerned with the fate of the Avon, after which C D Barwell commenced its salvation by purchasing for £1,500 the moribund Lower Avon Navigation Company Limited, carried out essential repairs and managed to keep the Navigation going until the Lower Avon Navigation Trust Limited was incorporated on August 1st 1950, with him as Chairman.

The renaissance of the inland waterways was under way!

After 1951 many major works were carried out and this colossal task was accomplished entirely by a voluntary organisation with money subscribed privately and with no assistance from government funds.

In 1962 the Navigation was re-opened to Evesham.
Behind this bare statement - the first successful venture of its kind in the world - can be imagined the enormous amount of time and effort of members and their supporters, and they, and generous donors, were responsible for preventing the Avon from reverting to its natural state - "a small mud-bound brook".

The Trust raised and spent hundreds of thousands of pounds on this work and it is now accepted, as a matter of course, that boats can journey between Tewkesbury and Evesham with ease and safety whilst most of their passengers, enjoying the passage and beauty of the river, are unaware that without the efforts of the Trust members and their supporters this would never have been possible.

C D Barwell, OBE died on the 6th October 1990 at his home overlooking the Avon. His vision and hard work over many years restored to the Vale of Evesham a priceless asset and inspired in others a resolve to undertake similar projects.

Spurred on by an anonymous donation of £¼ million to "prime the pump", the IWA led by Robert Aickman called a meeting of the Severn River Board, National Trust, LANT, Stratford Canal Society and other interested parties to consider the prospect of restoring the Upper Avon Navigation in order to re-connect the Stratford Canal at Stratford upon Avon with the Lower Avon at Evesham. This was under the chairmanship of Christopher Clifford and held at Thornbury Castle in Gloucestershire on 23rd November 1963 and, although support from certain quarters was not encouraging, a second meeting decided to hold further discussions to be arranged by LANT in the valley at Sammy Groves' Marine Ballroom beside the river at Evesham on 7th June 1964. This resulted in the formation by the IWA of the Upper Avon Committee under the chairmanship of Sir Fordham Flower. Subsequently it was decided that the Upper Avon Navigation Trust Limited should be formed and the Memorandum and Articles were duly formalised and signed on 26th August 1965. Eventually, due to the uncertain legal position regarding the Upper Avon Navigation, it was proposed to obtain a new Act of Parliament to enable work to commence and thus the Upper Avon Navigation Act was passed and became law in 1972.

It was understood that the extent and success of the operation would not be achieved using the LANT method of mainly volunteer labour with professional contractual support, so David Hutchings, MBE, who had successfully re-opened the southern section of the Stratford Canal under the auspices of the National Trust, was approached and offered employment with the Upper Avon Navigation Trust Limited as its Project Manager to undertake the refurbishment of the Upper Avon Navigation, which he accepted and successfully completed, with the grand opening in 1974 by H.M. Queen Elizabeth the Queen Mother on the "glorious 1st of June" at Stratford alongside Holy Trinity Church. The poet laureate, Sir John Betjeman, composed the poem overleaf to mark the occasion:

Stratford Holy Trinity Church

Inland Waterway

He who by peaceful inland water steers
Bestirs himself when a new lock appears.
Slow swing the gate: slow sinks the water down;
This lower Stratford seems another town.
The meadows which the youthful Shakespeare knew
Are left behind, and, sliding into view,
Come reaches of the Avon, mile on mile,
Church, farm and mill and lover-leaned-on stile,
Till where the tower of Tewkesbury soars to heaven
Our homely Avon joins the haughty Severn.
Sweet is the fluting of the blackbird's note,
Sweet is the ripple from the narrow boat.

Your Majesty, our friend of many years,
Confirms a triumph now the moment nears:
The lock you have re-opened will set free
The heart of England to the open sea.

Sir John Betjeman

Looking to the Future

It will have become apparent that at no time during the past 300 years has the Navigation been a profitable undertaking - always the revenue has been so small as to leave very little to spend on anything other than the sketchiest repairs - and never has it been possible to carry out properly the renewals and maintenance to resist the constant and insidious advances of Mother Nature. The river, always, is striving to revert to her natural state - a muddy brook in summer and a raging torrent in winter. Only by maintaining weirs and locks and keeping channels dredged can she be preserved for the benefit of man and the environment. By 1949 the outlook seemed bleak as all restoration attempts had been thwarted for so long by the river's unchecked natural tendencies. Ultimate disaster was averted when the Lower Avon Navigation Trust came to the rescue by raising and spending large sums of money to repair and restore what must still be considered to be "ancient works" and these are still exposed to all the ailments and decay of old age.

The largest proportion of the money was raised by thousands of donations and subscriptions from people concerned in preventing the Avon from becoming a muddy ditch.

With the river between Tewkesbury and Alveston restored, the continuing and continuous task of the Trust must be to administer, maintain and improve its properties, locks and navigation channels - all sheer hard, but essential work.

The Trust is a non-profit making company with the status of a charity and the future preservation and maintenance of the Navigation is dependent upon donations from the public to augment its toll income. Administrators of charitable trusts empowered to make grants in aid of causes such as this will be given every facility to see the work and workings of the Avon Navigation Trust upon application to the General Navigation Manager, Mill Wharf, Mill Lane, Wyre Piddle, Pershore, WR10 2JF.

The Trust welcomes new members and is always in need of volunteers for weekend lock-keeping duties in the summer months and physical work (painting, simple carpentry, site clearance, etc) on the Navigation. Those interested are asked to contact the General Navigation Manager in the first instance.

The Trust is a member of the Association of Inland Navigation Authorities (AINA)

Addresses and Telephone Numbers

Avon Navigation Trust

Mill Wharf Mill Lane
Wyre Piddle
Pershore
WR10 2JF
Office: 01386 552517
Wharf: 01386 556881

Avon Lock

Tewkesbury
GL20 5BE
01684 292129

Evesham Lock

Mill Bank
Evesham
WR11 4PP
01386 446511

Environment Agency Flood Line
08459 881188

British Waterways
The Dock Office Commercial Road
Gloucester GL1 2FB
01452 318000

Gloucester Lock, The Docks, Gloucester, GL1
2EH
01452 310832

Stourport Basin Stourport DY13 9EN
01299 829938

Diglis Basin Worcester WR5 3BW (BWML)
01905 356314

Diglis Lock (River Severn) Worcester WR5
3BS
01905 354280

Upper Lode Lock (River Severn)
Tewkesbury GL19 4RF
01684 293138

Stratford Canal (BW West Midlands Area
Office)
01926 626147

BW Emergency Telephone Number
08004 799947

Moorings in Tewkesbury

SUPPLIES AND SERVICES

	STRATFORD	WELFORD	BARTON	BIDFORD	HARVINGTON	OFFENHAM	EVESHAM	FLADBURY	WYRE	PERSHORE	ECKINGTON	BREDON	TWYNING	TEWKESBURY
BOAT SALES	•			•			•		•			•		•
BOAT REPAIRS	•	•	•	•			•		•					•
BOAT HIRERS	•			•			•							•
PETROL	•			•			•							•
DIESEL FUEL	•						•							•
BOTTLED GAS	•			•			•		•	•		•		•
MILK	•			•			•	•		•	•	•	•	•
BREAD	•			•			•			•	•	•	•	•
MEAT (Butchers)	•			•			•			•				•
GROCERY	•			•			•			•	•	•	•	•
GREENGROCERY	•			•			•			•	•	•	•	•
FISH & CHIPS	•			•			•			•				•
LAUNDERETTE	•			•			•			•				•
HAIRDRESSER	•			•			•	•	•	•	•	•	•	•
LUNCH & DINNER	•			•	•	•	•	•	•	•	•	•	•	•
BAR MEALS	•			•	•	•	•			•	•	•	•	•
MORNING COFFEE	•			•			•	•	•	•	•		•	•
PUBLIC HOUSE	•			•	•	•	•	•	•	•				•
HOTEL	•						•			•		•		•
POST OFFICE	•			•			•			•	•	•	•	•
NEWSPAPERS	•			•			•			•		•	•	•
SWIMMING BATHS	•						•			•				•

CHURCHES IN TOWNS AND VILLAGES NEAR THE AVON

CHURCH OF ENGLAND

TEWKESBURY
Abbey Church, Church Street 01684 850959
Holy Trinity, Oldbury Road 01684 292797
Priors Pk Chapel, Queens Rd 01684 298297
BREDON
St Giles 01684 772237
BREDON'S NORTON
Chapel 01684 772237
ECKINGTON
Holy Trinity 01386 750203
DEFFORD
St James, Harpley Road 01386 750203
GREAT COMBERTON
St Michael -
PERSHORE
Abbey, Church Row 01386 552071
WYRE PIDDLE
St Anne 01386 861203
CHARLTON
St Johns 01386 861203
FLADBURY
St John the Baptist,
Station Rd 01386 861203
CROPTHORNE
St Michael, Main Street 01386 861203
HAMPTON
St Andrew -
EVESHAM
All Saints 01386 442213
OFFENHAM
St Mary, Main Street -
MIDDLE LITTLETON
St Nicholas, School Lane 01386 830397
HARVINGTON
St James, Church Street 01386 870527
CLEEVE PRIOR
St Andrews, The Green 01386 830397
BIDFORD
St Laurence, Church Street 01789 772257
WELFORD
St Peters -
LUDDINGTON
St Margaret -
STRATFORD
Holy Trinity, Old Town 01789 266316

ROMAN CATHOLIC

TEWKESBURY
St Joseph, Chance Street 01684 293273
KEMERTON
St Benet's, Evesham Road 01386 725286
PERSHORE
Holy Redeemer, Priest Lane 01684 552737
EVESHAM
St Mary, High Street 01386 442468
BIDFORD
St Joseph, Quinney's Lane 01789 773291
STRATFORD
St Gregory, Welcombe Street 01789 292439

METHODIST

TEWKESBURY
Church Street 01684 298650
EVESHAM
Bridge Street
  01386 442380
BIDFORD
Chapel Lane 01386 438278
STRATFORD
Old Town 01789 298835

BAPTIST

TEWKESBURY
Station Road 01684 293044
PERSHORE
Broad Street 01386 556088
EVESHAM
Cowl Street
  01386 446368
BIDFORD
Salford Road 01789 491553
STRATFORD
Payton Street 01789 414205

QUAKER

EVESHAM
Cowl Street 01386 446552
STRATFORD
Maidenhead Road 01789 204331

Boat roped up to ascend Strensham Lock

The Mill Avon, Tewkesbury

TOURIST INFORMATION CENTRES

EVESHAM

Tourist Information Centre,
The Almonry,
Abbey Gate,
EVESHAM
WR11 4BG
Telephone: 01386 446944
e-mail: tic@almonry.ndo.co.uk
Internet: www.almonry.ndo.co.uk

PERSHORE

Pershore Tourist Information Centre,
Town Hall,
34 High Street,
PERSHORE
WR10 1DS
Telephone: 01386 556591
e-mail: tourism@pershore-tc.gov.uk
Internet: www.visitpershore.co.uk

Leaving the canal lock, Stratford upon Avon

STRATFORD UPON AVON

Tourist Information Centre,
Bridge Foot,
STRATFORD UPON AVON
CV37 6GW
Telephone: 08701 607930
e-mail: stratfordtic@shakespeare-country.co.uk
Internet: www.shakespeare-country.co.uk

TEWKESBURY

Tourist Information Office,
Out of the Hat,
100 Church Street,
TEWKESBURY
GL20 5AB
Telephone: 01684 855040
e-mail:tewkesburytic@tewkesbury.gov.uk
Internet: www.tewkesbury.gov.uk

Ferry in Stratford upon Avon

Bidford on Avon from the bridge

Stratford upon Avon riverside

Notes

Notes

Above Stratford Trinity Lock